Railway Carriage Album

G. M. Kichenside

LONDON

IAN ALLAN

Published by Ian Allan Ltd., Shepperton, Surrey and printed in the United Kingdom by Crampton & Sons Ltd., Sawston, Cambridge

Preface

ALL railway carriages look the same, so I was told on one occasion; yet there was as much if not more variety in coaching stock types on the many pre-grouping and the four group companies than in locomotive design. Yet it is always the locomotive that receives the greatest attention from enthusiasts. Nevertheless from the passenger's viewpoint, the railway carriage is the most important part of the train.

I have tried to portray a representative selection of stock from each of the major pre- and post-group companies from about the 1880s to the present day. Clearly space limits have not allowed the illustration of every type; indeed it was difficult to decide which photographs to omit. In some instances photographs of one company's stock will have to suffice to illustrate features common to several companies. Inevitably, too, there are gaps, and some companies are conspicuous by their absence, only because photographs of their coaches are no longer available except possibly in unpublicised private collections.

I have arranged the photographs in the order LMS, LNER, GWR, SR, LT, and BR with pre-grouping companies within their grouping successors, and the Album proper is preceded by a historical survey. The centre pages show a selection of carriage liveries reproduced to 3mm—1ft scale (TT gauge) in colour.

Finally I must acknowledge the assistance of those who have helped in the assembly of the photographs, particularly Messrs R. C. Riley, R. Chorley, D. L. Percival, H. C. Casserley, R. E. Wilson, T. J. Edgington, D. Cullum and the Public Relations Officers and their staff of the BR Regions and London Transport.

Woking, January 1966   G.M.K

Contents

Historical survey

TODAY, travel occupies a considerable part of our lives, both for pleasure and necessity. Speed and comfort are taken for granted; the modern train travelling smoothly with diesel or electric power at speeds of 90–100 m.p.h., with perhaps air conditioning, armchair seats, a restaurant or buffet car, or, if running at night, sleeping accommodation and the amenities—if not the space—of a good hotel, could not have been imagined 150 years ago when railways were in their infancy.

Railways were in existence at the beginning of the 19th century—indeed, records show that "rail" ways of a sort were known 200 years before this, but they were little more than local wagonways. The use of railways to carry passengers and general goods from one place to another on a commercial basis did not begin until the 1800s with the opening of the Surrey Iron Railway between Wandsworth and Croydon in 1804 for goods, and the Oystermouth Railway from Swansea in 1806 for passengers. Even then, the evolution of railways was slow and it was not until the successful development of the railway steam locomotive that commercial railways began in earnest, first the Stockton & Darlington in 1825, followed by the Canterbury & Whitstable and Liverpool & Manchester railways in 1830.

It was almost inevitable that the first railway carriages were virtual copies of contemporary road carriages and wagons, for the early railways were regarded by many only as a sophisticated form of road and it was not until about the late 1840s that railways diverged along their own form of development.

Travel in pre-railway days was not a part of everyday life, for almost everyone lived within walking distance of their work. Those who did need to move from one place to another, and who could afford to do so, travelled by stage or mail carriage, by post chaise, or on horse back, and the well-to-do had their own private carriages. Goods and, occasionally, passengers, travelled by wagon, which was sometimes covered but more often exposed to the elements.

The typical road mail carriage contained a single passenger compartment with transverse seats backing and facing the direction of travel. Generally the only windows were in the single swing doors on each side, and were capable of being lowered to provide ventilation; sometimes, however, windows were provided on each side of the doors as well. The side windows were usually shaped like a quarter circle or ellipse, thus blending with the turn under of the body ends. From their shape, or possibly because they were situated in the quarter of the body on each side of the doors, they were termed quarter-lights—a term still used today even though the quarter-lights are now four-cornered. The body sides were usually decorated with raised mouldings, dividing the sides into panels. Inside, coaches were often ornately finished, with padded seats and quilted body sides and ends. Some coaches had seats outside, alongside the driver, or at the back, and formed a sort of second class. Luggage was frequently carried on the roof, and mail coaches were equipped with a boot extending from the main passenger compartment. The mail guard sat on a seat either on top of the boot or on the roof of the coach.

Many of these features were found on some of the first railway carriages—the road coach style body with side doors and

7

quarter-lights, the mail boot, luggage on the roof and the seat for the guard, who now of course not only looked after the mail but had railway duties as well. Some railway carriages at first sported the liveries of the road coaches even to the extent of carrying fancy names. The essential difference lay in the fact that the railway carriage was longer than its road counterpart and contained two or three coach "bodies" or compartments mounted back to back, thus originating the typical British compartment carriage. Like its road predecessor, this style of carriage was only for first class passengers; second class passengers, those who would have travelled outside on the road mail coaches, travelled in a much more severe type of carriage, perhaps covered but often with open sides above the waist and with about three compartments containing wooden seats. Third class passengers, the lowest orders of the strictly class conscious society of the early 19th century, if indeed they were carried at all, were conveyed in what were

8

The first railway carriages were clearly derived from their road coach predecessors, like this mail carriage of about 1840. Notice the boot, the guard's seat, and the passenger seats on the roof. This particular example, however, has no quarterlights in the bodyside.
[Science Museum

little more than open goods wagons. Some third class carriages had wooden bench seats, and holes in the floor to let rainwater escape, but there was no protection from the elements or from the cinders thrown out by the locomotive. Several specimens from these early days of railways have survived and are preserved in one or other of the transport museums.

Most luxurious of the preserved relics is the bed carriage built in 1842 by the London & Birmingham Railway for the Dowager Queen Adelaide, widow of King William IV. This vehicle is little different from the standard mail carriages of the period, which contained 2½ passenger compartments and a boot at one end. In Queen Adelaide's carriage the boot was not used for mail but formed an extension from the adjacent passenger compartment. At night, stretchers placed across the gap between the seats supported an intermediate cushion and thus allowed the passenger to lie down lengthways in the compartment; the size of the compartment, however, was not sufficient for the passenger to lie full length between the partition walls and the bed was therefore extended into the boot.

From the 1840s

The poor travelling conditions of third class passengers in the early 1840s eventually attracted the attention of Parliament. Gladstone's Act of 1844 stipulated that third class passengers must be provided with covered accommodation and that all railways must run at least one train a day for third class passengers, at fares not exceeding a penny a mile at an average speed of not less than 12 m.p.h. The Act was open to liberal interpretations of what constituted covered accommodation. Some railways went to the other extreme in providing enclosed carriages containing few if any windows, perhaps not more than one door, and bench seats for about

60 passengers. Slatted ventilators sometimes provided the only source of light and fresh air. From this it will be apparent that the enclosed carriages were not divided into compartments, but were open from end to end. Gradually, however, the compartment-style interior was developed, with separate doors to each pair of bench seats which were divided by low seat backs. The advantage of this arrangement lay in the fact that only one lamp—if lighting was provided at all—was required for each coach. In first class coaches each compartment was usually, but not always, provided with its own lamp; sometimes a lamp would be placed immediately over the partition between two compartments and each would thus be lit by half a lamp.

From the description of Queen Adelaide's carriage it will be obvious that railway carriages in the early days were very small, little larger than road coaches, in fact, even though steam power, with its vastly increased haulage capacity over the horse, would have allowed the use of larger coaches. Ordinary carriages of the 1840s were about 20-25ft long, but no more than about 5ft wide and 5ft 6in-6ft high from floor to roof. The Great Western and its allied West Country companies, made full use of the extra width of the 7ft broad gauge which they had adopted, with coaches of about 24ft long, 9ft wide and 6ft high from floor to roof. Great Western broad gauge coaches were carried on six wheels from the start but coaches of other railways were generally on four wheels. Although some eight-wheeled coaches with a rigid wheelbase appeared early in railway development, they were isolated examples and eight-wheel coaches did not make a more general appearance until the 1870s. The wide body of Great Western first class coaches allowed eight passengers to be seated in comfort in each compartment. Some Great

Western first class compartments were sub-divided longitudinally into two halves with a communicating door between. Since at this time some Great Western first class compartments shared a single oil lamp with the adjoining compartment, the half compartments, therefore, received light from only a quarter of the lamp!

Unlike road carriages which could be stopped fairly quickly, a train needed a considerable distance in which to stop, for it was braked only by hand-brakes on the engine and on certain coaches. Brakes on carriages were worked by assistant guards positioned in the coaches concerned, for the brakes were not applied on every coach. The guards had to be able to see signals from the lineside or from the locomotive, so that they knew when to apply the brakes; for this reason, guards generally sat on a seat on the carriage end in such a way that they could see over the carriage roofs in front. In this position guards had to be careful to avoid overbridges, although there was ample clearance between the low roofs and the high overbridges designed to clear tall locomotive chimneys.

Stockton & Darlington first and second class composite of the 1840s which includes many features common on early railway carriages including the guard's seat and luggage rack on the roof, and the body compartment panels styled like those of road coaches.
[British Railways

Smoke and burning cinders thrown out from the locomotive were a nuisance and dangerous, and it was not long before train guards were placed inside special brake carriages equipped with observation positions so that they could still see signals. On some railways the guard sat inside an observation lookout built above normal roof level. This type of observatory, known as a lantern or birdcage, survived for many years, even after power braking was introduced, and its descendent, the periscope roof lookout, is a standard feature on British Railways today. Some companies adopted the side lookout—the well-known guard's ducket projecting from the coach side—but this has now gone out of fashion.

From the early days of railways, it was realised that mail could be carried more speedily by train than by horse-drawn mail carriage. Special carriages were built for carrying mail and were soon developed to allow mail to be sorted on the journey. As early as 1838 the Grand Junction Railway had a mail sorting carriage and, soon after, had developed apparatus to allow mail bags to be picked up and set down by a train travelling at speed. Although altered in detail, the basic pattern of train and lineside mailbag exchange equipment has changed little over the years and is still used today.

The mid 19th Century

By the 1860s the British railway carriage was beginning to look less like a road coach of 1800 and more like the railway carriage familiar to our own eyes—albeit very much smaller and shorter. Compartments had become established for all three classes of travel and, generally, differences between first, second and third class carriages lay in the size of compartments, and in internal appointments. Third class compartments were cramped and had nothing but bare wooden boards for seats and partitions which sometimes were taken up to the coach roof. Second class compartments were a little wider between partitions and seats and seat backs were usually padded and upholstered. First class was the height of luxury with well upholstered seats, arm and head rests, and quilted sides.

TOP LEFT: First class bed-carriage for Queen Adelaide, placed in service in 1842 by the London & Birmingham Railway. At night the bed, in the nearest compartment, extended into the boot.
[British Railways

RIGHT: A South Devon broad gauge first class coach of the late 1850s yet portraying such features as three-cornered quarter lights and body panelling turned up at the ends.

RIGHT: A standard gauge coach of the 1860s—a former London & North Western first and second class composite, seen here in later life in the service of a minor railway.
[Science Museum

LOWER LEFT: The interior of Queen Adelaide's bed-carriage, showing the bed laid on stretcher bars between the seats and extending into the boot on the left.
[British Railways

11

Lighting was still from primitive oil pots, shared between compartments in many cases; oil lamps themselves were portable and inserted through lids in the carriage roof into the lamp containers.

Although the compartment type of carriage was fast becoming established as the British standard, the saloon carriage, in which the passenger accommodation was in one large compartment occupying almost the entire carriage, had also made its appearance. Saloon carriages, which should not be confused with open third class vehicles, were usually for first class passengers and were of equal or better standard of accommodation to compartment firsts. Among the earliest saloons were the Great Western posting saloons of 1838. These broad gauge vehicles were unusual since the lower part of the body and the underframe were carried between the 4ft diameter wheels, but from about the waist the body was built out above the wheels to its full width. Seats were longitudinal, backing on to the bodysides; entrance to the coach was through a single central door. These coaches had clerestory roofs, the first railway application of this form of construction.

The clerestory, or "clear story", was of considerable antiquity in architecture, particularly in churches, and was employed to provide improved natural lighting. The raising of the central portion of the roof meant that windows could be fitted along the sides of the raised roof. In railway practice, the additional windows between the lower and upper roof sections were called decklights. Despite the early application of the clerestory to railway carriages it was not then pursued and did not reappear until the 1870s.

The saloon coach, too, was not widely employed for general use, and was developed more for private travel in the form of family or invalid saloons. Family saloons could be hired by the wealthy and attached to a train of their choice for conveying family parties, their luggage and servants between, for example, town and distant country residences. As railway carriages grew in size, the family carriage gradually developed

into a vehicle with one large saloon and an accompanying compartment for the servants. As their name implies, invalid saloons were employed for carrying passengers unable to travel in the normal way because of illness, but who were sufficiently wealthy to hire a private carriage. The main feature of an invalid carriage was a couch or bed which allowed the passenger to lie down. An attendant's compartment provided accommodation for servants or for a nurse accompanying the patient. A bed, or even a couch, in a railway carriage was still a novelty for the 1860s, and the only form of sleeping accommodation offered on night trains was the bed carriage arrangement, similar to that employed on Queen Adelaide's coach of 1842, and even bed carriages were not widely used. Indeed, mid-19th century passenger saloons were often the prototypes for amenities, as for example, heating, toilets, inter-coach communication and means of preparing food which, in later years, became a normal part of rail travel.

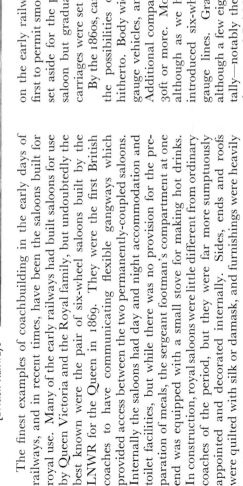

The finest examples of coachbuilding in the early days of railways, and in recent times, have been the saloons built for royal use. Many of the early railways had built saloons for use by Queen Victoria and the Royal family, but undoubtedly the best known were the pair of six-wheel saloons built by the LNWR for the Queen in 1869. They were the first British coaches to have communicating flexible gangways which provided access between the two permanently-coupled saloons. Internally the saloons had day and night accommodation and toilet facilities, but while there was no provision for the preparation of meals, the sergeant footman's compartment at one end was equipped with a small stove for making hot drinks. In construction, royal saloons were little different from ordinary coaches of the period, but they were far more sumptuously appointed and decorated internally. Sides, ends and roofs were quilted with silk or damask, and furnishings were heavily ornate.

Smoking was not permitted in trains or on railway premises on the early railways. The Eastern Counties was one of the first to permit smoking in its trains but only in selected coaches set aside for the purpose. The first smoking carriage was a saloon but gradually one or two compartments in ordinary carriages were set aside for smokers.

By the 1860s, carriage designers were beginning to appreciate the possibilities of making railway carriages larger than hitherto. Body widths were increased to about 8ft on standard gauge vehicles, and to 9ft 6in or 10ft on broad gauge stock. Additional compartments increased carriage lengths to about 30ft or more. Most railways still used four-wheel coaches, although as we have seen already the Great Western had introduced six-wheel coaches from the start on its broad gauge lines. Gradually other railways followed suit, and although a few eight-wheel coaches had been tried experimentally—notably the Great Western "Long Charleys" of 1852, the normal British carriage of the period was a four- or six-wheel vehicle. On the other side of the Atlantic the four-

13

and six-wheel coach was almost unknown and the normal American coach had eight wheels grouped together in two four-wheel trucks mounted towards the coach ends. The trucks, or bogies as they became known in Britain, were capable of turning on a pivot to follow curves in the track and generally gave a smoother ride than the rigid wheelbase of non-bogie vehicles.

The 1870s — bogie coaches

Bogie carriages in Britain did not make their appearance until the 1870s, at first in 1873 on the 1ft 11½in gauge Festiniog Railway; in the following years they were taken up by several main line companies, both in isolated experimental vehicles and in production batches, particularly on the Great Western and the Midland. The Midland in fact took the development a stage further by the introduction of twelve-wheel coaches mounted on two six-wheel bogies. Indeed, the years of the mid-1870s brought a considerable change in travelling conditions on the Midland, for not only were bogie vehicles introduced, but, following a visit to North America by the Midland's General Manager, James Allport, in 1872, the Midland introduced Pullman cars on a number of its services. But the most revolutionary change was the abolition of second class, the improvement of third class compartments to second class standards, including padded and upholstered seats, and the admittance of third class passengers to all trains. The Midland revolution naturally stirred neighbouring companies into the provision of better accommodation for third class passengers, although second class was retained and as part of a three class system did not start to disappear generally on other lines until the first years of the present century.

The introduction of bogies meant that the length of carriages was no longer limited by the length of a rigid wheelbase, itself restricted by track curves. Thus bogie carriages of over 50ft in length were developed—a considerable increase on short non-bogie vehicles. Nevertheless, not all companies welcomed the bogie vehicle and many would have nothing to do with it

at that time. Even the Midland continued building large numbers of six wheelers for main line use, and while the Great Western built bogie vehicles for long distance services, four-wheeled stock was employed on Great Western standard gauge local services. On the LNWR, Francis Webb, the Chief Mechanical Engineer, could see no advantage in the bogie arrangement; when longer coaches were contemplated on LNWR services, he adopted instead an eight-wheel arrangement in which the four centre wheels were mounted in axle-boxes rigidly secured to the coach solebars and the outer axles mounted in radial trucks which allowed limited side play. Some railways, among them the Metropolitan and the Great Northern, also used eight-wheel coaches, but the axle-boxes were rigidly suspended from the solebars although some of the axles were allowed limited side play to permit the negotiation of sharp curves. Although the radial and rigid eight-wheel arrangements were not widely adopted, specimens of both lasted for many years; although most of the LNWR radials were later rebuilt with bogies, a few survived in their original condition into LMS days. The LNWR radial eight-wheelers even then were not very much longer than six-wheel stock, for their length was standardised at 42ft over head-stocks, and rigid eight-wheel carriages of other companies were about the same length.

One of the earliest examples of Midland bogie stock was the 54ft clerestory-roof 12-wheel composite of 1876 built for Anglo-Scottish services; other Midland types included eight and 12-wheelers with and without clerestory roofs, and of various lengths. Thomas Clayton, the Midland Carriage Superintendent, did not employ the clerestory for long, and had reverted to arc roofs by the late 1870s until he revived the clerestory at the end of the century. William Dean on the Great Western, however, employed the clerestory for most Great Western main line stock from then on. The Dean bogie was also unusual in that the centre pivot bogie did not take the weight of the coach which was carried by four links

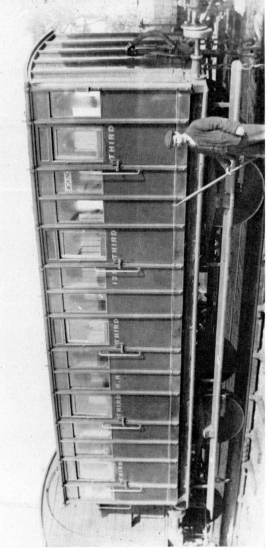

ABOVE: The mid-Victorian railway carriage gradually developed into a form familiar to our eyes; the Midland composite carriage of 1876 was notable for being among the earliest of bogie coaches. They were also among the first coaches to give third class passengers some comfort, following the abolition of second class by the Midland.
[British Railways

RIGHT: The other extreme was this Highland third of the 1870s which, apart from a smoking compartment, was open internally.

suspended from the coach solebars into mountings on the outside of the bogie frames, which were allowed sufficient freedom to permit the bogie to turn.

Pullmans

The Midland Pullmans, introduced in 1874, were themselves revolutionary when compared with the ordinary British carriage of the period. They were the largest coaches that had even run on a British railway, and were among the first British bogie coaches; but they were typically American in appearance, with end balconies and saloon interiors. The standard of accommodation introduced features hardly thought of in ordinary British coaching practice for it included the provision of heating, improved lighting, and toilet facilities, even for third class passengers. The cars were of several patterns and included parlours equipped with armchairs for daytime travel and sleepers for night travel. Pullman sleepers were laid out internally with both saloon and compartment accommodation. The sleeping berths in the saloons were formed from facing pairs of seats which were extended towards each other to form the berth; one of the occupants took what became the lower berth but the other had to use an upper berth—a complete bunk folded against the car roof during the daytime, but which at night was lowered to form the second berth above the lower one. Each pair of berths, or sections as they were known in Pullman parlance, were screened from the berths fore and aft by a portable partition mounted above the seat backs, and from the central passageway and the berths on the opposite side of the car by curtains.

In America, Pullman cars were not owned by the railway companies but were operated under contract from the Pullman Car Company which charged the passengers a supplement to use the cars. The Midland Pullmans similarly were operated under contract and passengers paid a supplement. Yet, despite their luxury, the cars were not an outstanding success; the complete trains of Pullmans were split up and cars were run singly in ordinary trains. Some cars were purchased by the Midland Railway from the Pullman Car Company and operated as Midland Drawing Room cars. Nevertheless, Pullmans appeared on other lines from time to time, notably the Great Northern, the London & South Western and the London, Brighton & South Coast, on which line Pullmans have operated almost without a break for over 90 years until the present time. The early Pullman cars themselves were built in America, dismantled for shipment and re-assembled in Britain at Derby. Later, a permanent Pullman Works was established at Preston Park near Brighton.

The Midland Pullman sleepers were not the first British sleeping cars although they were among the earliest. The first sleeping car proper as distinct from the bed carriage of the early railways, was a six-wheel vehicle built by the North British Railway in 1873 in which the beds were situated longitudinally in two large compartments. During the 1870s a variety of sleeping arrangements appeared, with berths or beds mounted longitudinally or transversely. One problem with the latter arrangement was the restriction of coach width, which was not quite sufficient to allow a 6ft long berth to be fitted across a carriage and leave space for a passageway or corridor as well. Some coaches had dormitories containing several beds side by side, and others had the Pullman arrangement of berths on each side of the saloon; on the Great Western, the wider coach bodies of broad gauge vehicles permitted transverse berths in compartments with a side corridor, the prototype in effect of the present day sleeper and first seen in the early 1880s. Most of the early sleepers had lavatory facilities, primitive though they were (and still are).

Developments of the 1880s

The 1880s saw the development of a number of passenger amenities on ordinary trains. Some ordinary coaches were equipped with lavatory facilities in toilet compartments placed between passenger compartments, although, even then, on most lines they were only for first class passengers.

In 1879 there appeared the first British dining car—a Pullman vehicle on the Great Northern Railway; in the next decade restaurant cars were introduced on other lines, particularly those to the north, but again they were only for first class passengers. The dining vehicles were still without gangway communication to adjacent coaches, and passengers either had to travel for the entire journey in the dining car or had to change carriages at an intermediate stop. Even this was preferable to the meal stops at principal stations which until then had been the only means of obtaining a meal en route other than by taking a packed meal. Even the packed meal contained in a luncheon basket could be quite sumptuous and could not be compared with today's sandwiches and a pork pie!

The Great Northern Railway took the provision of toilet facilities a stage further in 1882 when the company introduced the first ordinary British carriages with side corridors. The coaches concerned were short six-wheel first class and, later, third class vehicles, with, respectively, four and five compartments linked by side corridor to toilet compartments at both

ends of the coaches—one each for gentlemen and ladies. But still there was no access from one coach to another, for inter-coach gangways, apart from those on the pair of LNW Royal saloons and on a few Pullman cars did not make a general appearance until 10 years or so later.

Developments in carriage equipment were also becoming apparent by the 1880s. Among the most contentious were the various types of brake then in use. From the earliest days, hand brakes alone had been used, which had entailed the employment of guards distributed along every train to apply and release the brakes as needed. Various mechanical brakes had later been devised to allow the brakes to be applied on several adjacent vehicles or even throughout a train from one position which had the effect of providing additional braking power and reducing the need for guards or brakesmen. By the 1870s, power brakes of a variety of types and efficiencies employing compressed air, vacuum or hydraulic pressure, and mechanical brakes were in use, but most suffered by the fact that they were non-automatic and if the train became un-

17

coupled for any reason the brakes usually became inoperative on the detached portion. Following the particularly disastrous Armagh collision in 1889, railways were required by law to fit brakes that would be applied automatically on both or all portions of a train should an accidental division occur. Two forms of automatic brake became established from then on—the vacuum, which, as its name implies, utilises a vacuum in the train braking system to hold off the brakes which are applied by the admittance of air at atmospheric pressure to destroy the vacuum; and second, the Westinghouse compressed air brake, which used air under pressure to hold the brakes off and the release of compressed air from the continuous pipe through the train to apply them.

Lighting, too, was undergoing extensive development at this time. Simple oil lamps were still employed by many railways but from about the 1860s coal gas, carried in large

reservoirs on each coach or, in the case of set trains, in one or two coaches, had been used by a few companies. Others later opted for compressed oil gas which could be carried in compact cylinders under each coach and was generally less cumbersome. Electricity for lighting first made its appearance in a battery-powered Brighton line Pullman car in 1881. Experiments with generator-produced electricity were conducted on the LBSCR in the following years, and various systems of electric lighting with current produced by generators driven by belts from the coach axles were developed on other railways. Some companies, after initial experiments with electric lighting, returned to gas. Reasons advanced against the use of electricity were the better lighting then provided by gas, the additional weight of batteries and the drag caused by the dynamo belts which was claimed to affect locomotive hauling capacity.

Passenger alarm systems for use in an emergency were also being developed at this period. From the early days, engine drivers and guards used hand or engine whistle signals to indicate that the brakes should be applied, but as mechanical brakes were developed, with a consequent reduction in the number of guards on each train, the train guard generally rode at the back and a communication system between the guard and driver was almost a necessity. Thus developed the communication cord, which ran through the train from the guard to the driver. At first the cord was for use only by the train crew but, later, passengers were able to use the cord in an emergency. Sometimes the cord operated a bell on the locomotive or in a few cases operated a brake valve on the engine. Then, various electrically-operated alarm systems were developed which rang bells in the guards van and on the engine, but after the establishment of automatic power braking systems, the communication cord was confined within each coach and operated a valve connected to the automatic brake.

On the Great Western during the 20 or so years between 1870 and 1892 Brunel's 7ft 0¼in gauge had been giving way gradually to standard 4ft 8½in gauge. In readiness for the final changeover to standard gauge in 1892 when the West of England main line was converted, the Great Western had built large numbers of convertible coaches. Some had wide bodies which were narrowed by cutting a slice from the ends and partitions and pushing the sides closer together. Others had narrow bodies and broad gauge bogies in which the wheels came outside the solebars and were covered by a wide footboard. Thus, stock conversions involved changing bogies and, on some coaches, the narrowing of bodies.

The end of the century

The developments of the last decade of the 19th century brought the British railway carriage into the final stages of evolution; most of the features which today we take for granted could be found on carriages built towards the turn of the century, and subsequent development lay in improving materials and in details.

The two principal developments of the 1890s were the introduction of inter-coach gangway connections to provide access throughout the train, and in the development of dining facilities which were thrown open to all classes of passenger.

The Great Western took the lead in the introduction of the inter-coach gangway and the development of corridor trains, with a new corridor set introduced in 1892 between Paddington and Birkenhead. The gangways between the coaches were at the side of the coach and were in line with the interior side corridors. The side gangways were soon found to be impracticable since if a coach was turned the corridor was on the wrong side, and in later corridor trains on the Great Western, and on other railways which soon followed the Great Western's lead, the gangways were in the centre of the coach, even though the internal corridors were at the side of compartment coaches. Yet several companies, among them the Midland and companies in the south of England, were in no hurry to introduce corridor stock, for such vehicles seated fewer passengers than normal compartment coaches and would thus result in heavier trains and the need for more powerful locomotives. Many Great Western corridor coaches of this period, particularly coaches of all one class, were of the semi-open pattern with side corridor compartments and a small two- or three-bay saloon for smokers at one end.

The introduction of corridors through the train was accompanied by an expansion of railway dining car services, although the lead in this respect was initiated by the Great Eastern which extended dining facilities to third class passengers in a new three-coach dining-car set placed in service in 1891. The three vehicles were themselves linked by side gangways but were not gangwayed to the vehicles on each side. They were, moreover, six-wheelers, for the Great Eastern continued to build large numbers of four- and six-wheelers until the first years of the present century. Corridor trains with restaurant cars for all classes were introduced on the East and West Coast routes to the north in 1893, but the Midland, although following suit with third class diners, remained unconvinced of the advantages of through corridors for another few years. Passengers still had to travel in a Midland diner for the whole journey or else had to change carriages at an intermediate stop. The practice of travelling for the whole journey in Midland dining cars survived even after the introduction of through gangways, for it meant that a passenger on the longer journeys could take two or more meals at his own seat in the same way as in a Pullman car; the practice of reserving seats in dining cars continued through LMS days and was extended to other LMS dining car services; it still survives today on certain LMR dining car trains.

The Great Western side-gangway train was also notable for being one of the first fitted with steam heating fed from the

19

locomotive boiler. Until that time most coaches were un-heated; the few with built-in heating had stoves within, which in some cases were connected with hot water pipes around the carriage as in the case of the Midland Pullman cars. Other-wise coaches had no heat at all and passengers had to rely on footwarmers which could be hired for the journey at principal stations. Footwarmers contained hot water and sometimes sodium acetate, which had the property that if the footwarmer was shaken when cooling down, it could be persuaded to provide heat for a little longer than would otherwise have been the case. Footwarmers lasted until the early years of the pre-sent century, by which time steam heating had become general.

By the end of the 19th century the British railway carriage had developed from the short, rather cramped first cousin of the stage coach to a vehicle at its largest of about 65ft in length and 9ft wide, with corridors and through communica-tion, with restaurant facilities or sleeping accommodation, gas or electric light, heating and comfortable seating. That is what it could have been like on all railways, but it wasn't. Corridor trains were by no means universal on long distance services, and even the Midland, previously well to the fore in carriage design, placed a new non-corridor train on the St. Pancras-Manchester service as late as 1898. Despite the lead of the Midland in 1875 in abolishing second class, three classes still survived on some lines and particularly in the south of England and also on some services of the Great Northern, Great Eastern, the LNW, the Great Western and the smaller South Wales lines where wooden seat thirds not only still survived but were being built new.

The clerestory roof reached its peak at the turn of the century, particularly on the Midland-where Clayton had re-introduced it with an elliptical contour to both lower and upper decks in the mid-1890s – the Great Northern, North Eastern and the Great Western, on which it was employed for most ordinary coaches; a few other railways used it for such specialised vehicles as dining cars and saloons.

Electric lighting was being employed more extensively, but gas was still the main form of carriage lighting and the wide-spread adoption of electricity was a development of the early 1900s. Even oil lighting was still in use on some coaches.

Brakes on the other hand had been standardised on either the automatic vacuum or the Westinghouse air type. The adoption of two types of brake, however, led to some compli-cations particularly where through running from one railway to another was practised, as on the East Coast route where the Great Northern used the vacuum and the North Eastern and North British used the Westinghouse. Similarly on the West Coast route the LNW used the vacuum and the Caledonian the Westinghouse. Thus coaches employed on through services had to be dual fitted with both types of brake.

There was probably a more marked change in railway carriage development in the 1890s than at any time since the introduction of bogie stock in the 1870s. On the Great Northern, East Coast expresses, which had been formed of six-wheelers until about 1895 were transformed within about two years to trains of 12-wheel bogie stock with clerestory roofs and gangways throughout, which, while offering vastly improved passenger comfort, meant that train weights almost doubled. In fact it was limitations on load-hauling capacity of the small locomotives in vogue at the end of the 19th century that had to an extent imposed limitations on carriage weight. Carriage developments at the end of the century, which resulted in heavier trains, in turn brought about the introduction of larger, more powerful locomotives which naturally increased operating costs. Some of the smaller, less wealthy companies and, indeed, some of the larger ones as well, were naturally reluctant to introduce equipment that would be more expensive to operate.

Like many new types of railway equipment agreement could not be reached on a standard flexible gangway connection between coaches, and two basic types developed fairly quickly. One, the lengthy concertina or bellows type, was employed

East Coast Joint Stock third class dining saloon of the mid-1890s. This and a similar first class saloon were part of a corridor set train with side gangways, and which included a six-wheel kitchen car.

with the normal long-stroke buffers and screw couplings standard on practically all stock by the 1890s. It became known as the British standard gangway and was employed with detail modifications by most companies until the grouping and afterwards by two of the group companies. The other type of gangway, of American origin, became known in Britain as the Pullman gangway. It was wider than the British standard type and its main feature lay in the fact that it was normally employed in conjunction with automatic couplers later standardised as the buckeye type; the base of the gangway formed a solid buffing block above the coupler and side buffers were not needed. Pullman gangways were not coupled together but simply butted against each other and were held together by the rigid buckeye coupler. British standard gangways on the other hand were coupled by clamps on the sides of the gangway.

Pullman gangways and automatic couplers first appeared on British Pullmans in about 1888 on some vehicles placed in service on the East Coast route where Pullman gangways and automatic couplers first appeared in quantity and they were standardised on Great Northern and

East Coast Joint Stock corridor coaches from the late 1890s. Side buffers were also fitted, and the coupler head itself was designed to hinge out of the way to permit coupling to ordinary screw-coupled coaches Adaptors were also needed to couple the two types of gangway together because the rigidness of the Pullman gangway was of no use without automatic couplers. Although there were advantages in the automatic coupler and Pullman gangway, other companies refused to have anything to do with them and it was not until the 1950s that they became standard for all new stock.

The 1890s saw the opening of the pioneer deep-level underground railways in London and the Liverpool Overhead Railway which demanded specialised types of rolling stock. Underground services were not new, for the Metropolitan and the Metropolitan District railways in London had been running since the 1860s but their rolling stock had been little different in principal from that of the main line companies. From the start the new tube railways were operated by electricity with the motive power provided either by electric locomotives as on the City & South London or by electric motors built into the passenger coaches themselves as on the

21

Waterloo & City, which introduced the electric motor coach type of vehicle. But because of the confined space inside the tube tunnels, compartment-type carriages with side swing doors were impracticable, for there would be no means of escape if a train should break down between stations. Thus the open saloon type of carriage with entry through end platforms came into use for this type of service. Because of the fire risk, metal was adopted wherever possible in place of wood.

The Edwardian era—1900

From 1900, steel and other metals were used increasingly in carriage construction by the main line companies, particularly for underframes, where vehicles of 60ft or more had outgrown the length for which wooden solebars were practicable.

From then on, passenger coach design was more closely allied to the type of service on which the stock was employed. Non-corridor compartment stock was of bogie or four- or six-wheel types, although bogie stock was becoming predominant on steam suburban services; cross country and the shorter-distance main line services were generally provided also by non-gangwayed stock, some of which would have lavatories between compartments or short internal corridors connecting groups of compartments to toilet facilities. Long distance trains by now were mostly provided with corridor stock and many trains had restaurant cars. The Great Central had introduced that most useful of refreshment vehicles, a buffet car, containing a bar counter to serve light refreshments, on some of its London services from the opening of its main line to Marylebone in 1899.

Although railway carriages had almost reached their maximum length, and width, too, in some cases, full advantage had not always been made of the height limits. Some companies, it is true, had adopted the clerestory, the top deck of which virtually reached the maximum height permitted by the loading gauge, but carriages with plain roofs, more often than not still had low arc roofs, no more than 1ft higher in the centre than at the sides. A few companies had developed a semi-elliptical roof profile, fairly steep at the sides but almost flat on top. From 1905 the high elliptical roof, which took advantage not only of the full height permitted by the loading gauge, but provided more space inside the coach at roof level than was given either by the clerestory or arc roof, first made its appearance on the Great Western and Caledonian railways and was soon taken up by other companies.

Indeed, in 1905 the Great Western placed in service the largest railway carriages ever built for a British railway then or since. From their size these coaches gained the nickname 'Dreadnoughts' from the Battleships introduced at about the same time. The Dreadnought coaches were 68–70ft in length over headstocks and 9ft 5in wide over body. An unusual feature was the staggered corridor which changed sides half way along the coach; also unusual and in advance of its time was the internal layout whereby the compartments could be entered only from the corridor, and passenger access to the coach was by end and centre doors instead of by doors to each compartment. This arrangement was evidently not thought to be popular for the Great Western reverted to individual doors to each compartment in succeeding designs and the end door coach did not re-appear on the Great Western for about another 30 years. Yet despite their size the Dreadnoughts weighed no more than about 33–34 tons.

The Caledonian coaches, too, were the largest ever to have run on that railway—65ft long and 9ft wide over body, for weights of from 35 to 38 tons according to type. These coaches, known as the Grampian stock, were carried on six-wheel bogies, although the longer Great Western Dreadnoughts were mounted on four-wheel bogies. The Caledonian Grampians were placed in service between Aberdeen and Glasgow/Edinburgh, and for their time were quite luxurious, with electric lighting, steam heating and compartment sizes which, in the third class at least, put the Great Western to shame. The Grampian thirds varied between 6ft and

The largest coaches ever to run in Britain were the GW "Dreadnoughts" built in 1905, which had bodies 9ft 6in wide and 70ft, or so, in length. They were among the first to have a high elliptical roof; because of their size they were more or less confined to former broad gauge routes of the GWR.
[The late G. H. W. Clifford, by courtesy P. J. Garland

6ft 4½in between partitions, but the Great Western Dreadnought thirds were no more than 5ft 6in. In 1906 the Caledonian placed some similar non-corridor 12-wheel coaches on its Glasgow-Edinburgh services. Thereafter, however, the Caledonian standardised 57ft long coaches on four-wheel bogies for both corridor and non-corridor stock.

Nigel Gresley, the newly-appointed carriage and wagon superintendent of the Great Northern Railway also introduced the high elliptical roof on new stock built for the Kings Cross-Sheffield service in 1906 after a prototype had appeared on a Great Northern railmotor the year before.

The LBSCR also employed a high elliptical roof for some of its main line stock built at this time, but soon reverted to the low arc roof which it retained until the end of its existence. Other railways retained the lower flattened elliptical roof, as for example the SEC, LSW and LTS, while the LNW employed this form of roof intermediately between the low arc roof of the turn-of-the-century stock and the high elliptical roof introduced on that line in about 1907. The Midland on the

other hand retained the clerestory roof for its main line stock and used a rather low elliptical roof for its suburban stock. It was also still building new stock with gas lighting, and so, too, did the Great Northern, Great Western and a few other companies, although all had some vehicles with electric light.

Another type of coach known by the name "Dreadnought" was the new high roof 54ft stock of the Metropolitan, first seen in 1905 and built in batches for Aylesbury line services until about 1921 and in multiple-unit form for about another 11 years after that. These Metropolitan main line coaches anticipated present day practice, for although they were purely non-corridor side-door suburban carriages, some third class compartments were connected in threes by a centre passageway through the partitions. This feature was later abolished and normal partitions segregated each compartment. Three Metropolitan Dreadnoughts are preserved on the Keighley & Worth Valley Railway.

Previous Metropolitan steam coaches, known as Ashbury stock, built between 1896 and 1900 were short, narrow, bogie

LEFT: Soon after the turn of the century the Great Eastern embarked on a programme to widen its 8ft wide stock to 9ft, which increased seating capacity by 20 per cent. A coach is seen here split down the middle before the new framing and panelling were spliced in.

vehicles, 38ft long and 8ft wide, with low arc roofs. Many were converted for use in electric multiple-unit trains from 1905; six coaches of this type, reconverted for steam haulage, survived on the Chesham branch until 1961 and four are still active on the Bluebell Railway.

In the early 1900s, suburban trains serving large cities, particularly in South and East London, were still composed mainly of four-wheeled stock, close-coupled in long rakes of up to 15 or more vehicles. A number of companies, however, introduced bogie vehicles for suburban work from this time and non-bogie stock gradually went out of favour.

It was during the early 1900s that several companies realised that wide-body stock could hold more passengers for little increase in carriage weight. A standard five-compartment 8ft wide third class carriage of the period could seat 50 passengers but a 9ft wide coach could seat 60. The Great Eastern, which carried the country's heaviest suburban traffic, had introduced wide body suburban stock in 1899; to bring its earlier 8ft-wide stock up to the same capacity the Great Eastern performed a widening operation on the narrow bodies by slicing them lengthways along the centre and splicing in new floor, end and partition panels and widening the seats. Because of the critical limits of the loading gauge, the bodysides were slightly inclined to provide a 9ft width at cantrail level but only 8ft 10in at the waist, which with new grab handles alongside the doors and recessed footboards provided an overall width of 9ft 11in. The coach side frames at seat level were reduced in thickness from 3½in to 2in to

LEFT: Two styles of Midland coachbuilding: nearer the camera is a Clayton vehicle with toplights, square-cornered mouldings and clerestory roof, standardised between 1895 and 1905. Beyond is a Bain coach with low elliptical roof and round-cornered mouldings employed from about 1908.

[British Railways

provide extra seat width. Other companies with wide-body four-wheelers included the Great Northern, which had recessed doors to maintain the limits of the loading gauge, and the LBSCR, which built one train of wide-body stock so restricted by loading gauge limits that no further sets were built.

At the same time the LBSCR introduced 8ft wide bogie stock on some services and from 1903 the LSWR introduced its four-coach bogie block sets which within a few years had replaced all non-bogie stock on London suburban services. The LTSR had introduced bogie coaches of generally similar profile to its four- and six-wheel stock on its Southend expresses from about 1901.

In later years the Great Eastern, too, introduced bogie vehicles for suburban work, but to avoid scrapping four-wheelers still with more years of useful life, four-wheel coach bodies were mounted in pairs on bogie underframes. Some coaches were thus widened and lengthened over a period of about 15 years.

Three classes of travel were still common on London suburban services. Third class carriages were normally very austere with wooden or woven wire seats; second class compartments normally had upholstered seats and the interiors were slightly less spartan and the first class were of ample proportions, with well upholstered seats, head and armrests, and they were provided with a carpet.

The same years also saw the development of the first suburban electrification by main line companies. In 1903 came the Mersey Railway conversion from Liverpool Central to Rock Ferry, and the first Metropolitan District electric experiments in London; 1904 saw the Lancashire & Yorkshire's Liverpool-Southport and the North Eastern Railway's North Tyneside lines and in 1905 came the general Metropolitan and Metropolitan District schemes in London. They were followed by the Midland's Lancaster, Morecambe & Heysham electrification in 1908 and in the following year by the LBSC South London line scheme from Victoria to London Bridge.

All these companies except the LBSC opted for open saloon stock, with entry through end platforms. Some at first used folding gates to enclose the platforms but, soon after, the platforms were enclosed as entrance vestibules with sliding or swing doors. The Mersey Railway stock was unusual in having inward opening swing doors. The coaches on the Lancashire & Yorkshire's Southport electric line were notable for their flat sided 10ft wide bodies and the two-and-three seating in the third class saloons. The first District Railway stock had end gates but a form of power-worked sliding doors in the centre of each car. The latter were not successful and hand worked sliding doors were employed on the District for the next 30 years; the last hand-worked doors in fact survived until the mid-1950s. The stock for all these electrified lines was of the multiple-unit pattern in which all the electrical equipment and traction motors were carried on the coaches. Each set contained one or more motor coaches and was provided with driving cabs at both ends, either in motor coaches or driving trailer cars. Several units could be coupled together and driven from the cab at the leading end, a feature which soon proved its worth in simplifying operating techniques.

The LBSCR used compartment-type coaches for its electrified services although the coaches for the initial South London line had an internal side passageway within each coach. Despite the earlier difficulties with wide-bodies, the South London coaches were unusual for the LBSC in having 9ft wide bodies but they were confined to one route on which the loading gauge was not quite so restrictive as on other parts of the LBSCR. Later LBSC electric stock reverted to a body width of 8ft. Aluminium made its appearance in the external body panels of the LBSC stock and in the Liverpool-Southport trains.

Three electrification schemes were inaugurated during the first years of the 1914–18 war which had the effect of releasing steam locomotives urgently wanted for use on freight services. The LNWR introduced electric traction on its North-west London suburban lines in stages between 1914 and 1922, the

LSWR converted some of its London suburban lines which formed the beginning of today's great Southern electric network and the Lancashire & Yorkshire electrified its Manchester-Bury line. Clearly opinions still varied on what was considered to be the most suitable type of suburban electric coach, for the LSWR, following the example of its neighbour, adopted compartment stock; in fact the new three-car LSW electric sets were formed by conversions from the 1903 four-coach bogie block steam sets. What became motor coaches were rebuilt with new distinctive V-nosed front ends. The LNW introduced new open saloon three-car trains, gang-wayed within each set. The trains were of two types with different electrical equipment and detail body variations; there were only four sets of one of the types with Siemens' equipment, which were originally placed in service on the Willesden-Earls Court line; re-equipped, these units survived until 1966 on the Lancaster, Morecambe & Heysham line. The other LNW sets, with Oerlikon equipment worked the Euston-Watford and Broad Street-Richmond services. The Lancashire & Yorkshire also used saloon sets for the Bury line; they were similar in many respects to the Southport trains of 1904 but were of 9ft 2in width and had high elliptical roofs; they were of all-metal construction, one of the first such examples in main line practice.

Meanwhile, the first decade of the present century saw the development of the deep-level London tube railways. Here, too, open saloon stock was used, with entry through open end platforms protected by gates. Gatemen were employed on the trains to control the gates at stations and each man dealt with the pair of gates on adjacent car ends. Gates lasted for much longer on the tube railways than on surface stock because hand-worked sliding doors were not permitted on the tube lines. It was not until the successful development of air-worked sliding doors in the early 1920s which could be controlled throughout the train by one guard, that gates finally succumbed. Not all tube stock had gates; the joint stock

delivered in 1920 for the London Electric and London & North Western through Bakerloo-Watford service had inward-opening swing doors which could be locked while the train was running between stations. Each coach still needed an attendant but he could control all the doors along the car sides from one position. These sets were built specifically as a compromise for tube and main line suburban service and the floors were slightly higher than standard tube stock to allow for the difference in platform heights of tube and surface stations. These cars were not altogether successful and within about 10 years had been displaced by ordinary tube stock which worked through to Watford.

Multiple-unit operation was standardised on tube lines although at first the Central London and the pioneer City & South London railways employed electric locomotives. The Metropolitan Railway also used electric locomotives for hauling its Aylesbury line trains over the electrified lines as far as Harrow (Rickmansworth from 1925) where steam locomotives took over.

In 1905/6 many companies introduced steam railmotors in attempts to reduce operating costs on some lightly used services. The Great Western was first in the field in 1903 and soon had almost 100 self-propelled coaches. The advantage of a rail motor was that it was powered by a small steam engine unit which was far more economical in fuel than even the smallest tank engines normally in use on local and branch services. Since the coach was self contained there were no engine shunting movements at the end of the journey and at branch terminus stations the facilities could be very simple. The open saloon pattern was adopted internally which permitted the issue of tickets on the train by a conductor/guard and thus allowed a reduction in operating staff.

Railmotors generally fell into two groups—those with the engine unit enclosed within the coach body in an engine compartment, and those with a separate engine unit to which the carriage body was attached by an articulated coupling,

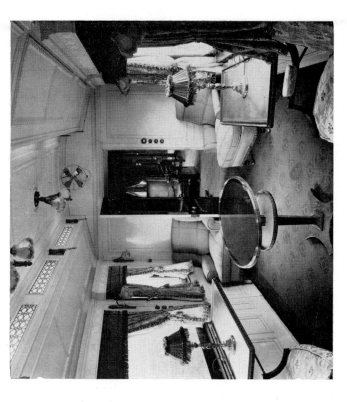

ABOVE: The two Royal saloons built by the LNWR for King Edward VII and Queen Alexandra in 1903. RIGHT: The day compartment of King Edward's saloon. Both saloons are preserved at Clapham Museum. [British Railways

the opposite end being mounted on a normal bogie. Some steam railmotors were designed to haul trailers, but most of them were underpowered for this sort of work. In fact, it was the inflexibility of the railmotor in coping with periods of heavy traffic that led to its downfall. From it was born the push-pull train which employed a normal tank engine coupled to two or three ordinary coaches, the outermost one of which was fitted with driving controls to allow the driver to operate the regulator and brake. When the engine was pushing the train, the driver rode in the leading coach but the fireman stayed on the engine to attend to the fire and water. There were also a few isolated experiments with petrol-engined railcars at this time but they were not notable by their success.

The Edwardian years saw a marked improvement in standards of accommodation on main line stock and, in many respects, the peak of British coachbuilding was reached in the years before the first world war. Certainly the elegance of some of the designs, the standard of craftsmanship in construction and the luxurious appointments of some first class coaches and special saloons were never quite attained after the first world war, or after grouping, as mass production techniques and the economics of rail travel demanded more rapid construction, the use of new materials and more austere finish and decor.

Undoubtedly among the best vehicles of the early 1900s were the two Royal Saloons built by the LNW in 1903 for King Edward VII and Queen Alexandra. In appearance they followed the practices of the LNW and West Coast Joint Stock diners and saloons of the period with clerestory roofs and ornate panelled bodies. Internally the Royal coaches had day and night saloons, a smoking saloon and dressing rooms. The LNW formed a complete Royal train by the addition of dining cars and a number of semi-royal family saloons, which could be fitted up for day or night use for the entourage, and two brake vans for luggage. The LNW Royal train was normally employed when the entire Royal household had to be conveyed, as for example between Windsor and Balmoral. In 1908/9, the East Coast partners also built two Royal saloons, one by the North Eastern Railway and one by the Great Northern. They were more modern-looking than their LNW counterparts for they had elliptical roofs, but internally their appointments were similar if, perhaps, less ornate.

The Great Northern and the London & North Western railways both built some special corridor trains during this period. The Great Northern trains were 12-wheel four-coach sets for the Kings Cross-Sheffield service in 1906 and were among Gresley's first designs as carriage superintendent of the Great Northern. In the following year the LNW placed in service a special set for the Euston-Liverpool American boat trains. It was an eight-coach formation of uniform appearance throughout (unusual in LNW practice) with high elliptical roofs and ornate body panelling only used before on sleepers, diners and saloons. Most of the coaches were 12-wheeled. In 1908 similar coaches were introduced on the afternoon service between Euston, Glasgow and Edinburgh.

Also unusual for the LNWR was the use of a separate kitchen car on the Liverpool boat set, a gas-lit 50ft vehicle from which meals were served into the adjoining dining saloons. The remainder of the train was electrically lit, but the kitchen car necessarily carried gas for cooking. The train sets for the "Corridor", as the afternoon Euston-Glasgow service was known, did not include new dining cars, and older clerestory-roofed diners were included in the formation. Like the morning trains, the Glasgow and Edinburgh portions each contained their own restaurant cars.

The provision of restaurant facilities varied from line to line, and the type of cars provided depended largely on the number of meals that would be served. Usually where numbers were small and could be served conveniently in two or three sittings, one vehicle, containing kitchen, first and third class accommodation, would suffice. The Great Northern Sheffield four-coach sets included a composite restaurant car, and the Great Western later used composite cars on its services. Often the kitchen was in the centre of the vehicle with the third class saloon at one end and the first class at the other. The LNW and the Midland on the other hand usually needed more than one dining vehicle, the former on its heavier Liverpool and Manchester services and the latter, not because its trains were heavy, but because of its practice of allowing passengers to travel in the dining car for the whole journey as I mentioned earlier. Thus a first class car with kitchen was usually paired with a full third saloon, or, if the first class clientele was in a higher proportion, a kitchen third would run with a full first diner although at that time this formation would be rare, for expense account business travel had not developed then to the extent that it has today. Just after the turn of the century the Lancashire & Yorkshire had produced a most curious dining vehicle for its Fleetwood boat train, an open brake second with a kitchen. If that combination wasn't sufficiently unusual the Lancashire & Yorkshire made sure that it was unique, for it was a ten-wheeler with a six-wheel bogie

The dining cars built in 1901 for the L&Y's Leeds-Fleetwood boat train. On the left is an open first; on the right is the unique ten-wheel kitchen brake second, with its part-clerestory roof over the kitchen. [British Railways

under the kitchen and a clerestory roof over it, with a plain arc roof for the remainder.

Sleeping cars had developed to the type of vehicle that we know today by the early 1900s, although in some respects the fittings were more elaborate. Most cars, which were still for first class passengers only, usually contained eight or nine single berth compartments with transverse beds or bunks and sometimes a double berth compartment with two side-by-side beds, and a side corridor. Some sleepers contained a normal compartment with seats for the use of passengers who wished to smoke before retiring, for smoking was not allowed in sleeping berths. The Midland which had employed Pullman sleepers from the 1870s continued with the Pullman open saloon arrangement for many years; even in 1900 the Midland placed in service some sleeping cars built by Pullman in America and assembled in England, which retained the traditional Pullman interior layout with a large general saloon and longitudinal lower and upper berths and private compartments. But by 1906 the company was building its own sleepers of what had become the traditional British side corridor compartment type.

Most types of sleeping and dining car were carried on six-wheel bogies because of the smooth ride which the latter provided. As we have already seen, six-wheel bogies were used on a number of ordinary coaches, in some instances only because the short locking bars then in use at many facing points would have been bridged by four-wheel bogies on the longer coaches. The other use of six-wheel bogies was solely for the better riding characteristics, but their use on ordinary stock was limited and four-wheel bogies became the accepted standard.

Although Pullman-owned cars had ceased to be used for night journeys, day Pullman parlour cars with and without kitchens were used on a number of lines, particularly in the south of England where they were common on the LBSCR. The new Pullman train placed in service on the "Southern Belle" between Victoria and Brighton in 1908 was distinguished by having elliptical-roofed stock, the first Pullmans so built. Pullmans made spasmodic appearances on a few other lines; the Metropolitan had two cars on its London-Aylesbury and Chesham line services and the SEC and LSW had a few cars; later they spread to the GE, Caledonian and to Ireland but Pullmans did not find widespread use on other lines. Some companies would have nothing to do with them and even the

29

Midland and the Great Northern, where some of the pioneer Pullmans had run, did not pursue the venture.

The years before the grouping

In 1911 the Midland placed in service some new suburban stock which, while not in advance of its time, laid the foundations of Midland and, later, LMS suburban stock design for the next 30 years. The coaches were short, no more than 50ft in length but had 9ft wide bodies, thus allowing six-a-side seating inside, were gas lit and had low semi-elliptical roofs. Most vehicles were actually 48ft long over body and were of a number of types ranging from brake thirds and thirds to full firsts, and some were provided with inter-compartment toilets. The Midland "City" sets employed between Moorgate and various Midland suburban stations were of this pattern and similar 13-coach sets, though with electric lighting and Westinghouse brakes, were placed in service on the LTS line to Southend in 1915.

The Great Western also built some special City sets in 1919 which resembled the Midland sets in some respects, particularly in length, although they were only 8ft 5½in wide and thus seated five-a-side in the thirds. In 1911 Gresley produced the first of his articulated sets for Great Northern London suburban services. The first eight-coach trains were formed of two-coach units but later examples were articulated in fours as "quad-arts". The Great Northern sets, like the Midland, were gas lit, but there the comparison ended, for the Great Northern vehicles internally were far inferior to those of the Midland. Third class compartments were no more than 5ft 3½in between partitions compared with the Midland's 6ft and the seats were sparsely upholstered. The object was, of course, to carry as many passengers as possible and, on the short journeys, comfort was not of prime importance.

Yet the construction of non-bogie stock had not ceased even then, for in 1910 the LNW built some new four-wheel sets for the North London Railway's Broad Street–Richmond service.

Except for length—the third class coaches were 30ft and the firsts 28ft—they were similar to current LNW bogie suburban stock, with high elliptical roofs, but were equipped with coalgas lighting and liveried in North London varnished teak. At about the same time the LNW built some six-wheel suburban sets for its Birmingham area services and as late as 1923 the Caledonian placed in service some new four-wheel bogie sets, similar to its latest bogie suburban vehicles, for the Balerno services from Edinburgh.

At the other extreme in commuter services were the "club" saloons employed on certain trains. They were more common on longer distance business trains on Lancashire & Yorkshire and LNW services to the Manchester area particularly from Blackpool, Southport and Llandudno. Special vehicles were provided, with first class appointments and usually in the form of a saloon. A small pantry provided liquid refreshment, particularly welcome for the tired businessmen returning home after a hard day at the office. Travel in the saloons was confined to those who belonged to the club and paid a sub-

30

LEFT: Ashford Works, 1907. Under construction are some of the corridor brake tri-composites, built for through working between Kent Coast stations and the Midlands and North of England. [British Railways

RIGHT: Midland suburban coaches of 1911 laid the foundations of later Midland and LMS stock for the next 30 years. Nearest the camera is a Midland 48ft brake third with high elliptical roof, built for the LTS line in 1920; beyond is an LMS 54ft third of the mid-1920s. [G. M. Kichenside

scription for the privelege to a club committee who thus guaranteed to the railway company a full load of first class passengers in the coach. Each member usually had his own seat which he occupied day in, day out. In the South, the LBSC ran a first class saloon and a first class corridor coach (one of the very few corridor coaches on the LBSCR) on its "City Limited" first class only train between Brighton and London Bridge. Many SECR coaches included saloon compartments, particularly in the later three-coach "Trio C" sets which when used on business trains had a club atmosphere, even if it was not on an organised basis.

The four years from the end of the 1914–18 war to the grouping in January 1923 saw the last designs of the pre-grouping companies. The ordinary British main line carriage by this time was a vehicle of about 50–60ft in length with side corridor and end gangways, with compartments having external side doors on the compartment side. Open stock was unusual except on suburban and underground electric carriages, and for dining purposes. Suburban steam stock was purely of the non-corridor compartment type but the longer distance suburban trains were usually made up of stock including between-compartment toilets or with short internal corridors to such facilities. Gas lighting was on the way out—gradually —and electric lighting was standard on practically all new stock. Steel was being used in carriage construction, particularly for underframes, and some companies were using steel sheets for body panelling instead of wooden panels and mouldings.

The Midland Railway at last gave up the clerestory roof from about 1917, and adopted the high elliptical roof for both main line and suburban stock for the last years of its existence. Just before the grouping, two of the South Country railways, the LSWR and SECR, introduced new corridor stock; the LSW steel-sided high roof coaches gained the name "ironclads" and the SEC 62ft flat sided matchboarded vehicles were known as the "Continental" stock. These SEC 8ft wide vehicles were quite unlike anything previously built on the SEC; entry was through end doors only and the high elliptical

31

roofs prevented the use of a birdcage lookout, with which most previous SEC brake vehicles had been equipped, and the flat matchboarded sides gave the coaches a curious un-British appearance.

The Great Western had also used steel panelling for body-sides although its coaches were still fully lined out in panelled style. The Great Western also adopted maroon livery from about 1910 but evidently thought better of it and reintroduced chocolate and cream with some new 70ft stock built for the South Wales-London service in 1922. Great Western coaches built between 1905 and 1919 were distinguished with toplight windows above compartment quarter lights and over large corridor windows. On the Great Northern, too, many coaches had toplights above the ordinary windows but gradually the toplights were merged with the main windows to form one deep window light reaching to cantrail level.

On most other lines designs current in about 1910–15 were continued with little change right up to grouping. Great Eastern stock was fairly standardised on a few basic types, nearly all about 50ft long, for main line and suburban duties. New Great Eastern third class suburban coaches still retained low back partitions, and although the compartment arrangement was adopted, coaches were open from end to end inside. The Great Central had introduced new stock in 1912 which although only 60ft long and 9ft wide was of rather massive appearance with a balloon roof. A later feature of these vehicles was an anti-telescoping device—a horizontally-toothed casting built into the coach ends which, in the event of a derailment, was intended to prevent one coach riding up over its neighbour. But whether or not the device was called on for a practical test, it was later removed.

The Scottish companies continued until grouping with existing designs, although the North British had placed in service some all-steel dining cars and the Glasgow & South Western had introduced two rather ornate 12-wheeled restaurant cars; one had a high-elliptical roof and a low clerestory

roof above it, with coloured glass decklights in the sides.

1923—The grouping

Although there was some continuity of carriage and wagon design after the grouping in that the carriage and wagon chief or the chief mechanical engineer of one of the constituent companies was appointed to head the same department of the group company in all four cases, only on the Great Western was there a direct continuation of design. Indeed, Great Western carriage design did not alter much for the next decade or so, and the standard main line carriage continued to be of the side-door pattern until the mid-1930s. There were variations in detail, particularly in width, for the generous loading gauge bequeathed by the broad gauge allowed the use of coaches with bodies as wide as 9ft 6in on certain routes. After a final batch of 70ft stock built in 1924 Great Western coach lengths became standardised at 57 or 60ft for ordinary vehicles. Suburban stock of purely compartment type (the Great Western did not build any non-corridor stock with toilets after the grouping or, for that matter, for some years before the grouping, either) generally followed the same pattern as corridor stock except that the normal width was 9ft or, at the most, 9ft 3in. Many suburban coaches for both London and Birmingham areas were formed into four coach sets, some of which were close-coupled. For main line stopping services and certain branches the Great Western built large numbers of two-coach non-corridor sets, both vehicles brake composites with one first among the third class compartments. For other branches the Great Western built its saloon pattern auto-trailers for push-pull operation, which were descended in concept from the original steam railmotors of 1903–10.

Collett, the Great Western's Chief Mechanical Engineer, also experimented with articulated coaches on some main line sets and for additional "City" sets for the London area, but the idea was not pursued and the corridor coaches were later rebuilt with individual bogies. The Great Western also tried

Pullman-type gangways and buckeye couplers on some coaches but decided to retain side buffers, screw couplings and British standard gangways for the future.

Although Gresley of the Great Northern was appointed as Chief Mechanical Engineer of the London & North Eastern, his LNER designs seemed slightly less massive than their Great Northern predecessors, even though teak construction, varnished teak livery and domed roof ends on corridor stock were continued. Among the first LNER non-corridor coaches were some quad-art (four-coach) and quint-art (five-coach) articulated sets respectively for the Great Northern and Great Eastern suburban lines. The latter followed Great Eastern practice in that they were fitted only with the Westinghouse brake. Both types were generally similar and resembled Gresley's previous Great Northern articulated London suburban sets but with detail modifications including electric instead of gas lighting.

The normal LNER main line corridor coach was a teak-bodied vehicle, generally 60ft long, although some corridor coaches were only 51ft in length, with side doors to each compartment; Pullman type gangways and buck-eye couplers were standard items. A feature of LNER practice was the construction of set trains for some of its crack expresses as, for example, the "Flying Scotsman" and "Hook Continental", both of which were re-equipped in the mid-1920s.

For local services non-gangwayed coaches, usually 51ft long, both with and without toilets, were built, and many were articulated in pairs. Gresley made extensive use of articulation except for ordinary corridor stock, where more-flexible train formations made articulated sets less desirable. Nevertheless, following a complete five-car articulated dining car train built for the Kings Cross-Leeds service in the last years of the Great Northern's existence, Gresley built several triplet dining sets for main line service and some sleeping-car twin sets. The Great Northern quintuplet restaurant set featured electric cooking in the kitchen car, powered by batteries under

the car and supplemented by mains land-line connection at each terminus. Subsequently Gresley standardised all-electric kitchens on LNER restaurant cars.

By the early 1930s the LNER turned to the end-door design for its corridor stock; like the LMS, the LNER also built a large number of open coaches for ordinary service. The LNER remained wedded to teak-bodied construction until the end of the 1930s, even though steel-panelled stock had been used by the other companies for a decade or more. This was not blind conservatism, for wood was still cheaper than steel, and teak bodies needed nothing more than an occasional coat of varnish which helped to preserve the natural oil in the wood. Yet steel had to come, and in about 1938, following experiments a few years before, came the first ordinary LNER coaches with steel body panels.

On the LMS, R. W. Reid the Midland Carriage Superintendent continued in that position and it was hardly surprising that Midland designs were perpetuated. Yet they were not purely Midland, for, on corridor stock at least, the LNW standard length of 57ft was adopted rather than the Midland's 54ft; non-corridor stock was built to both lengths depending on its area of operation. Although steel was used for underframes, the LMS decided very firmly to continue with wooden-bodied coaches for the first years of its existence to the extent that Reid reorganised Derby Carriage Works to turn out wooden-bodied stock on mass production methods. Yet the LMS did not entirely ignore the possibilities of steel construction and in 1926 ordered over 200 all-steel passenger coaches and about 300 full brakes from outside contractors. Yet despite the form of construction—they were truly all-steel with steel frames, body and roof panels—passenger coaches weighed no more than about 30tons compared with the 27tons of comparable wooden-bodied stock.

The all-steel passenger coaches were of the open pattern with end doors, which started the trend towards open third class vehicles for ordinary travel. At the same time the LMS built large quantities of wooden-bodied open vehicles with end doors. Ordinary side-corridor coaches still had side doors to each compartment, but by 1927 end-door side-corridor coaches had been introduced on the LMS. These and the open coaches were unusual in having two windows to each seating bay or compartment, a practice which could be traced back to the Midland's Clayton dining cars of about 1900. Large single windows to each bay or compartment appeared soon after and were unusual in British practice for the entire window could be lowered in the same manner as on European stock. Ventilator windows employing rotating glass vanes were fitted above the main window and could be adjusted by the passenger to face or trail the airstream. At the same time a composite form of construction employing timber body frames and steel panelling was introduced which remained standard almost to the end of the LMS in 1947.

LMS coach design underwent a radical change in the early 1930s. New constructional methods in which the window glass was secured from inside the coach meant that the steel bodysides were completely flush and neater in appearance than hitherto. The large windows to compartments or bays had rounded corners and instead of lowering the main window for additional ventilation, as on the stock of 1928–30, sliding window ventilators were provided in the upper part of the frame. LMS non-corridor stock changed little except for the transition from wooden panelled bodies to the steel, flush-sided type. There were no new set trains even for such services as the newly-named "Royal Scot", although this train was distinguished by a first class lounge brake, which included arm-chairs in a large saloon, and by some semi-open first class vehicles seating only two-a-side in the compartments. The LMS continued to use gas for cooking in kitchen and

In 1926 the LMS placed in service over 200 all-steel open thirds and open brake thirds (left) although at that time continuing to build large quantities of wooden-bodied stock, typical of which is the corridor first (right).

[British Railways; G. M. Kichenside

BELOW RIGHT: The LMS employed gas for cooking and lighting in most of its full kitchen cars; but two cars built in 1933 were fitted with diesel-electric generators and electric stoves. One was included in the "Royal Scot" train which toured North America in the same year.   [British Railways

restaurant cars until the end of its existence, although two all-electric kitchen cars powered by built-in diesel generators were constructed in 1933; one was included in the "Royal Scot" train which toured North America in that year.

The LMS built large numbers of vehicles for use in three-coach general-purpose inter-district sets of corridor, non-corridor and non-corridor lavatory types. There were also sets built for specific suburban services as, for example, the five coach sets (which unusually included a 51ft composite—the shortest LMS passenger vehicles ever built) for the Cathcart Circle in Glasgow and occasional 11-coach sets of 54ft stock for the Fenchurch Street-Southend line.

On the Southern Railway, Maunsell, who had come from the SECR, started afresh in carriage design and produced a range of corridor types which remained unchanged, except in detail, for the next 15 years. They were mostly on 58ft underframes and of composite construction with timber body framing and steel sides. Side doors were retained for compartments but some open vehicles with end doors were also produced, mainly, although not exclusively, for dining purposes. Pullman type gangways and buck-eye couplers were adopted as standard features.

The Southern was hampered by loading gauge restrictions, particularly on former SEC lines; those from London to Folkestone and Ramsgate could take coaches no wider than 8ft 6in over body, while the Tunbridge Wells-Hastings line was severely restricted by Mountfield tunnel to stock no wider than 8ft over body for stock of about 60ft in length. Thus Maunsell built his standard coaches to three widths—9ft, 8ft 6in and 8ft—for general use in the first case and for the restricted lines in the other two. The Southern did not need to build any steam non-corridor coaches, for it inherited large quantities of non-corridor stock from its three constituent companies. The SEC had built large numbers of 60ft 10-compartment thirds anticipating later conversion to electric operation, but although the electrification of former SEC lines was inaugurated in 1925 the 10-compartment thirds remained unaltered, and the Southern obtained most of its suburban electric stock in the 1920s and 1930s by rebuilding earlier pre-grouping stock from all three constituents. Many of the conversions were from SEC four- and six-wheel coaches mounted in pairs or in parts on new bogie underframes. However, the Southern did build two batches of new suburban electric stock in 1925 for its Eastern and Western section electrifications, generally similar in style to its corridor stock but with 8ft 6in wide bodies. The two batches differed in detail; the Western section motor coaches had V front ends like the original LSW electric sets and the coaches in the Western Section sets were shorter (motor coaches 57ft, trailers 60ft) than their Eastern Section 62ft-long counterparts.

In 1932 came the first of the Southern's main line electrification schemes, that from London to Brighton. Stock for

stopping services consisted of four-car units, each coach 62ft long and 9ft wide but with recessed sides for the guard's and driver's compartments, like Maunsell's SR 9ft wide steam stock. Three coaches in each unit were non-corridor; the fourth coach, a trailer composite, had an internal side corridor connecting all compartments to end toilets. Six-car units were provided for express services, gangwayed through the unit but not at the driving ends. The motor coaches were of the open pattern with doors at the ends of the saloons but the trailer cars were of the side-door type and were generally similar to contemporary steam stock. Length was standardised at 62ft 6in and width 9ft. The original Brighton line express sets included a single composite Pullman car in continuance of the Brighton line Pullman tradition. Three all-Pullman five-car electric multiple-unit trains were built to work the "Southern Belle"—soon renamed "Brighton Belle" to avoid confusion with other South Coast "Belle" Pullman trains introduced by the Southern.

Later six-car sets for the Eastbourne and Hastings electrification did not have Pullmans, but one of the trailer firsts in each unit included a pantry for the service of light refreshments. These sets normally ran paired with a six-car Pullman set as 12-car trains.

For the later main line electrification schemes the Southern adopted four-car express units with gangway connections at the driving ends so that up to 12-coach trains could be gangwayed together with access throughout the train to the restaurant or buffet car which was usually included in one of the units. For stopping services on these lines the Southern opted for two-car units, some with internal side corridors in one or both coaches; other sets were purely non-corridor two-coach suburban type units which had been converted from former LSW steam coaches.

By the time of the grouping in 1923 second class had been abolished on so many lines that it was virtually extinct, and first and third class became the normal British standard.

Pockets of second class survived however; on SEC lines of the newly-formed Southern Railway second class was still in use on ordinary trains for a few months after the grouping but was soon suppressed by the SR authorities, and second class accommodation was provided on GE and GN suburban services of the LNER until about 1938. On SEC stock there was a clear difference in standards of accommodation for all three classes, both in compartment dimensions and in internal decor and appointments. SEC thirds normally seated five-a-side, seconds four-a-side and firsts three-a-side. On the LNER GE and GN quint and quad-art sets second and third class compartments were identical in size and about the only difference, apart from the fare, was the provision of a carpet in the seconds. Second class accommodation continued to be provided on Southern and LNER Continental boat trains to match the three class system employed on European railways.

In 1928 came a notable development which removed the final traces of Victorian class consiousness in the provision of travelling facilities, the introduction of sleeping cars for third class passengers—a long overdue innovation. They appeared on all three railways operating sleeping car services, for the Southern, alone, did not have any sleeping cars. The accommodation was by no means luxurious and was standardised at four-berth compartments with two lower and two upper berths in each. Each bunk, for they could not be called beds, was equipped only with a rug and a pillow and provided nothing more than lying down accommodation. But it was a start, and ordinary travellers to Scotland or to the West of England could at least attempt to sleep, cramped though the accommodation was. Although the austere rug-and-pillow berths have since been superseded on British Railways, the arrangement is now used extensively on the Continent in what are known as couchette coaches, containing six berths to a second class compartment (four in the first class); a 12-compartment coach can thus sleep 72 passengers.

During the 1920s steam railcars once again made an

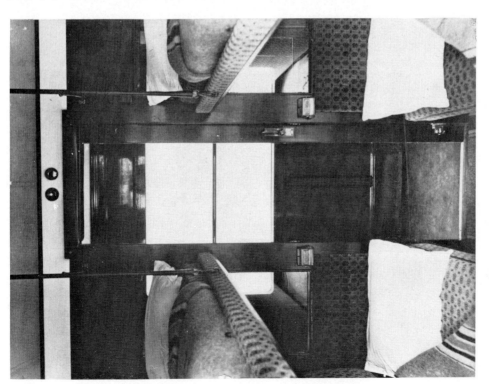

One of the last major additions to British railway facilities, the third class sleeping car, was introduced in 1928. Each compartment contained two lower and two upper berths, all equipped with a rug and pillow. [British Railways

appearance, particularly on the LNER. The main difference from those of 20 years earlier was in the engine units which, although powered, employed gear drive and were similar in some ways to an internal combustion engine. But once again they did not prove entirely successful and, although a few of the LNER cars lasted for about 20 years, the push-pull train continued in popularity for many branch services.

Also at this period there were further experiments with internal-combustion-engined railcars of both petrol and diesel driven types. The LMS produced a four-car diesel-electric unit converted from Lancashire & Yorkshire electric coaches from the Bury-Holcombe Brook line, but it was not entirely successful. Nevertheless, the break-through to satisfactory diesel operation was on the doorstep, and by the early 1930s the LMS had placed in service the first of its diesel shunting locomotives. In 1933 the Great Western produced the first of its AEC-engined diesel railcars, of which 38 were eventually built. These cars were used on main line and branch services; some had toilet facilities and a few had buffet counters. Highlight was an inter-city express service between Birmingham and Cardiff operated by a single third-class-only car, for which a supplement of 2s 6d was payable, but the popularity of the railcar proved its undoing and it had to be replaced by an ordinary train. The early cars could only work singly, but later units, which had more angular bodies than the earlier streamlined cars, were more powerful and were equipped to haul trailer coaches.

During the 1930s the LMS and LNER introduced new electric multiple-unit stock for their electrified suburban lines. The LMS adopted compartment-type coaches for new stock to supplement the existing trains in the London area and on the Liverpool-Southport/Ormskirk lines, between 1927 and 1933. But by 1938 the LMS had changed its concept of suburban electric stock by introducing open saloon pattern cars with air-operated sliding doors for the Wirral electrification and a year later for the Lancashire & Yorkshire replace-

ment stock on the Southport line. Both types were of light-weight all-metal integral construction in which there was no separate underframe and the coach body was self-supporting. As a result the Southport stock, although among the largest in the country—66ft 6in long and 9ft 3in wide—weighed no more than 24 tons in the case of the trailer cars and 41 tons for the motor coaches compared with the 28 tons and 56 tons respectively of previous LMS compartment electric stock. The Wirral stock was also very light but it was of smaller dimensions than normal main line stock.

The LNER used the open saloon arrangement for its North Tyneside replacement stock but the coach bodies, of normal composite timber and steel construction, were provided with hand-worked end sliding doors and were articulated in pairs.

Special trains 1935-9

In the mid-1930s special sets were placed in service for some named trains of three of the four companies. The Great Western and LNER led the way in 1935 with trains for the "Cornish Riviera Limited" and new "Silver Jubilee" respectively. The streamlined "Silver Jubilee" train was formed of articulated twin sets and a triplet dining unit. Particular attention was paid to internal and exterior decor and the train was liveried in silver and grey. The steel body panels were taken down to cover solebars and underframes, and rubber fairings covered the space between coaches. The Great Western "Cornish Riviera" trains were notable for their width, 9ft 7in over body. In profile they were similar to some special saloons built for Ocean Liner boat trains in 1931. The coaches were of the end-door pattern, but because of the width the doors were recessed. The doors were unusual since they were hung to open towards the coach ends; thus those at the left hand ends opened to the left, the reverse of normal practice.

In 1937 the LMS introduced new sets for its "Coronation Scot" trains although the coaches themselves were not new and had been adapted internally in seating and decor from

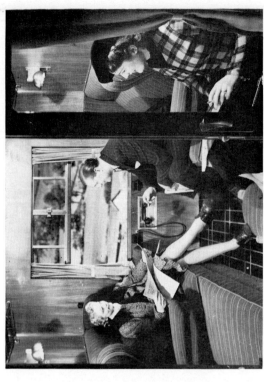

ordinary vehicles. The LNER built new sets at the same time for its "Coronation" and "West Riding" trains. They were similar in concept to the "Silver Jubilee" but were formed entirely of articulated twin sets. Internally the "Coronation" and "West Riding" trains were open throughout and passengers were served with meals at their own seats, Pullman fashion. In the following year the LNER introduced new set trains for the "Hook Continental" and "Flying Scotsman" trains but they had the normal teak bodies similar to ordinary LNER stock, included side corridor accommodation and were not articulated. Finally in 1939 the LMS, evidently not satisfied with its 1937 "Coronation" sets, which were rather inferior to their LNER "Coronation" rivals, produced part of a new "Coronation Scot" train formed of articulated twin sets of semi-integral construction and with more modern —if rather jazzy—decor and such gimmicks as telephones in each compartment direct to the dining car. To publicise the train the LMS sent it on a tour of North America for the World Fair in New York but war broke out in September 1939 and put an end to the running of the high speed streamliners and marooned the 1939 "Coronation Scot" train in America until 1946. The LMS in fact completed the delivery of new stock for three "Coronation Scot" sets in 1946/7 but in the event the train was not restored; the articulated twin sets with their non-standard seating layout which would have upset seat reservation arrangements on normal services were relegated to relief and excursion duties and to Manchester area long distance commuter trains.

The LMS also employed semi-integral construction methods for ordinary main line stock in some articulated excursion trains built in 1938. Each train was formed of five articulated twins, all of open stock including an open composite in one set. But again, all-metal and integral construction were not

generally pursued and, by 1939, the timber-framed steel-panelled type of body was virtually standard on all four group companies.

London Underground stock in the 1920s and 1930s

The London Underground railways and the Metropolitan—which was as much a main line company as the LTSR on the other side of London had been until it was taken over by the Midland in 1912—were not included in the grouping of 1923 and remained nominally independent for another 10 years when the London Passenger Transport Board was formed to take over all of London's road and rail public passenger transport. As we have already seen, rolling stock for the deep level tube lines changed little until the advent of a successful air-operated sliding door in the early 1920s, after which, the end gates on tube cars were quickly replaced. Trailer cars at least were provided with more door space than before with two sets of double sliding doors on each side. Motor cars had only one set of double doors but part of the car body was taken up by equipment carried above floor level. In view of the severe consequences of a train fire in the confined space of underground tunnels wood was eliminated as far as possible in tube stock and all-metal construction was adopted at an early date.

On the sub-surface lines, however, hand-worked sliding doors continued in use on open saloon stock and air-doors did not appear until 1935, after the formation of the LPTB, on some new stock for the Hammersmith & City line, only to be converted to hand-operation when the cars were transferred to the District line three years later. Meanwhile, in an attempt to combine the best features of open saloon and compartment coaches the Metropolitan experimented with an electric multiple-unit set known as the "hustle train", built in 1920 with open saloon interiors but side swing doors at intervals along the coach side. This arrangement was not entirely successful and in 1921 the Metropolitan built another batch of normal open stock but with three sets of double hand-worked sliding doors along the sides of each car. This was the last open stock built for the Metropolitan and all subsequent multiple units for the Rickmansworth and Watford services, were of the compartment type, similar to the "Dreadnought" locomotive-hauled compartment coaches built between 1905 and 1921 for main line services to Verney Junction. Some of the compartment motor coaches were equipped with vacuum brakes and were capable of working with "Dreadnought" trailers.

A feature of Metropolitan open saloon stock motor coaches was the inclusion of a luggage compartment between the driver's compartment and the passenger saloon. The compartment motor coaches also lost passenger space by having the electrical equipment carried above floor level.

District electric stock, however, always had its equipment carried under the floor which allowed most of the space in motor coaches to be devoted to passenger accommodation.

The design of District multiple-unit stock did not alter radically in the 1920s; clerestory roofs were retained on new stock until the end of District's separate existence but additional doors were provided on later stock. There was, however, one important exception, the 1920 stock which was quite unlike anything built for the District until then or afterwards. The 1920 sets were of massive all-steel construction which gained them the nickname "tanks", and were the widest stock on the Underground network, 9ft 6in over body panels. They were of open saloon pattern with sets of double hand-worked sliding doors along the sides; uniquely, they had elliptical roofs and the car ends had oval windows. Most of the seats were arranged longitudinally along the bodysides, thus leaving plenty of room for standing passengers. The "tank stock" was the most powerful on the District and, unlike other District sets, which were a haphazard collection of cars of varying vintages, was always maintained in complete units. They ended their days on the Metropolitan line in the early 1960s. A small batch of tube stock of similar construction, including oval end windows, was ordered in 1919 and was notable for being the first tube stock to have air-worked doors throughout.

After the formation of the LPTB in 1933 some experimental tube stock designs appeared in 1936 before a standard was evolved for future construction. At the same time a standard sub-surface design was adopted which was unusual in having the coach sides flared outwards at solebar level, which prevented a foothold unless the sliding doors were open. Open saloon interiors, air-worked sliding doors and equipment carried on the underframe were adopted as standard features on both tube and sub-surface stock. Nevertheless, in 1938 when the new types first appeared, compartment stock, including some of the original Metropolitan Ashbury short bogie stock of 1898 worked many of the Metropolitan line services. On the inner London sub-surface lines of both Metropolitan and District, older saloon-pattern stock, usually with hand-worked sliding doors, survived in profusion. Some

After the second world war the LMS again tried all-steel construction for some of its coaches. Seen above is a completed corridor composite, and, below, a vehicle under construction. Some of these coaches, distinguished by their round "porthole" windows, were not completed until after Nationalisation in 1948.

[British Railways

of the designs looked rather antique and many vehicles had clerestory roofs—indeed, the last clerestory stock for the Underground—the Hammersmith & City sets already noted—was delivered as late as 1935, 30 years after the clerestory began to be abandoned on main line stock.

The end of the group companies—1945-7

Like the period after the first world war, the years following the end of the second world war in 1945 provided an opportunity for the development of new designs, but once again another grouping—this time Nationalisation, on January 1, 1948—heralded more sweeping changes and more standardisation. Yet in the three years between, each of the four companies produced stock that showed marked changes over pre-war designs. The LMS post-war coaches were little different in general layout to stock of the late 1930s, but the LMS once again opted for all-steel construction for some batches of new stock. An unusual feature distinguishing post-war LMS corridor stock was the provision of a circular window

41

semi-corridor composite.

in the toilet compartments and in the corridor side opposite toilet compartments, which gave the coaches concerned the nickname "porthole" stock.

Great Western post-war corridor coaches too were not very different in layout from pre-war stock but a new feature was the sloping end to the roof on corridor stock, rather like the domed roof of Gresley LNER coaches. Although Great Western post-war corridor vehicles were of the end-door pattern, some compartments retained external side doors as it was claimed by the Great Western that some passengers preferred direct access to the compartment. The Great Western provided one or two doors along the corridor side to supplement the end doors. This meant that corridor side windows were not equally dispersed and narrower windows flanked each of the middle doors. Following a few serious train fires the Ministry of Transport Inspecting Officers recommended the provision of additional doors on the corridor side of end door stock belonging to all companies where this was practicable. The LMS thus cut additional door spaces between the large corridor window lights although in fact not all LMS end-door corridor stock was so altered.

The post-war corridor coaches of the LNER designed under Thompson, Gresley's successor as Chief Mechanical Engineer, were of a completely new pattern. The most notable feature was the attempt to overcome some of the difficulties inherent in the traditional British end-door side-corridor coach by the spacing of the external doors part way along the coach body on both sides so that to reach any compartment it was not necessary to pass more than one other compartment—a great improvement for passengers carrying luggage. The coaches themselves, 6ft 6in long, were of composite wood and steel panelled construction, and the "varnished teak" livery was painted on the steel panels. Another distinguishing feature on LNER post-war coaches was the oval-shaped toilet window. Thompson also introduced a range of non-gangwayed coaches, both of purely non-corridor types and one type of

But the most marked change in coaching stock design occurred on the Southern. O. V. Bulleid, who had pioneered many innovations in locomotive matters, was in command when the first coaching stock developments appeared, not in post-war days but in 1941 when the first suburban electric stock to seat six-a-side was introduced. For many years the Southern had been beset by loading gauge restrictions which prevented the universal use of 9ft wide stock. In pre-war years many of the track tight spots had been eased and by the end of the 1930s it was possible to use wide-body stock on all London suburban routes. In the first 9ft wide suburban electric stock, coach bodies were steel-framed with external steel panelling. The coach sides were of minimum thickness at seat level to provide the maximum width internally where it was most needed. The first few Bulleid suburban electric sets included some 11-compartment trailers seating 132 passengers, the highest seating capacity of any British stock before or since with the exception of the unique double-deck train of 1949.

Post-war Southern suburban stock was less austere, compartments were not so cramped and the open saloon arrangement was introduced although side doors were retained to each seating bay. There were differences in body design, for post-war stock was of all-steel construction and had a full front end without the domed roof. The first Bulleid stock still retained a wood and canvas roof with a domed end over the driving cabs at the outer ends of the set. The saloon seating introduced the five-a-side (two and three on each side of a passageway) seating arrangement to the Southern Region, although it had been seen before on both the Lancashire & Yorkshire and LMS Liverpool-Southport stock and on Great Western diesel railcars. Distinctive features of the bodyside were the round-cornered windows, and toplights in doors.

After an initial batch of steel-bodied side-door main line stock, similar in many ways to the post-war suburban electric stock, Bulleid introduced some new main line stock which, in

Nationalisation

On January 1, 1948, the four group companies were nationalised under the name British Railways, but for the first three years there was little change in carriage design, for the existing company types continued to be built for the regional successors. One outcome, however, was the production at Swindon of a batch of Great Western design non-corridor composite coaches for the London Midland Region since the LMR's own carriage works could not undertake their construction. Other changes affected liveries and allocation, where lines were transferred from one region to another. A particular case was the Fenchurch Street-Southend line which was transferred with its LMS coaching stock to the jurisdiction of the Eastern Region.

The Southern continued to turn out steel-bodied electric stock, most of which was built on reconditioned underframes recovered from withdrawn wooden-bodied electric stock. It will be remembered that the Southern Railway had obtained much of its suburban electric stock in the 1920s and 1930s by mounting old bodies on new underframes. Now those underframes were given new all-steel bodies at a cost considerably below that for completely new coaches, for the old underframes had many more years of life before them.

It was at this time, too, that the Southern felt the full effect of the vast post-war increase in the number of passengers travelling to and from London in peak hours. The reduction in working hours meant, moreover, that the peaks were more sharply defined and concentrated in a shorter period in the morning and at night. The considerable overcrowding on some Southern suburban services, particularly in South East London, clearly demanded extensive remedial action. The Southern therefore experimented with a double-deck suburban electric unit in an attempt to increase the carrying capacity of an eight-car train. The restrictions of the British loading gauge meant that the coaches were not true double deckers, for the upper compartments were interlaced with the lower

many ways, set the pattern for future stock throughout British Railways. The new coaches were 64ft 6in long and were of the end-door pattern although most types had intermediate doors and a transverse vestibule about half way along the coach. Many of the coaches were of the open pattern and some brake thirds included both open saloons and side corridor compartments. Nearly all steam stock on the Southern was formed into numbered sets—the only one of the four group companies to employ set formations extensively.

There were many detail developments on the SR's post-war stock; for example, leather window straps to hold door drop-windows had long since been abandoned on the Southern Railway and replaced by locking levers in the immediate pre-war stock and by frameless balanced windows in post-war vehicles.

Among other detail fittings that had disappeared generally over the years were lower footboards, a relic of low platforms at one time fairly common at some country stations. While automatic slam locks had come into general use on most coaches by the 1920s the Great Western had reverted to the non-automatic lock which required the handle to be turned to open or close the door. Surprisingly, this type of lock was used on some of the post-war vehicles and means that even today staff must pay particular attention to the doors of these surviving Great Western vehicles to ensure that the doors are closed and the handles turned.

During the years of the Grouping the attitude towards smokers altered completely. Gradually the amount of smoking accommodation was increased; eventually smoking was permitted in any compartment not labelled "non-smoking", the reverse of previous practice. By 1947 the proportion was normally one non-smoking compartment for every four to six smokers; in recent years, however, by public demand the trend has gradually reversed and on some lines the proportion is now about equal, but on London Transport trains non-smoking accommodation is now greater than smoking.

ones in such a way that the upper deck seats protruded into the lower deck roof space. Each high level compartment was connected to its neighbouring lower deck compartment by a short staircase.

But the train was not an unqualified success because in practice it took longer for the higher number of passengers in each pair of compartments to board and alight, and the train lost time at stations. The Southern did not pursue the idea and instead embarked on a costly programme of train lengthening, which meant the provision of additional stock, longer platforms and resignalling. Nevertheless the Southern Region's double deck train survives as an interesting and unique venture. It is interesting to recall that on the LMS Stanier had drawn up plans in the late 1930s for double-deck suburban stock of the open pattern for the St. Pancras-Bedford service but they did not come to fruition. The Southern Region's double-deck train was notable for the fact that it was the first unit on the Southern Region to be equipped with the electro-pneumatic brake, a development of the Westinghouse air brake applied and released electrically. This form of brake had first appeared as long ago as the early 1930s on London Underground stock and had since been employed on nearly all London Transport stock and by the LMS for its Liverpool area stock of 1938 and 1939. It is now standard on all new electric multiple-unit stock on both British Railways and London Transport.

In 1949, the LNER inaugurated the electrification of the Liverpool Street-Shenfield suburban service, for which it introduced three-car multiple-units which normally worked as nine-car trains. Following pre-war LMS practice the open saloon layout with air-operated sliding doors was adopted; some similar stock was introduced on Manchester-Glossop suburban services when the former Great Central line between Manchester and Sheffield was electrified in 1954.

The Shenfield electrification at last allowed the withdrawal of most of the surviving Great Eastern suburban stock, the

last of which dated from about 1920. But British Railways had not finished with it yet; a severe steel shortage curtailed the construction of new coaches. The old Great Eastern Shenfield vehicles, which had steel underframes, were rebuilt with new bodies of generally LNER Thompson pattern but of unique design to match their 54ft length and employing reconditioned material where possible. Four types of non-gangwayed coach were produced, two of which included toilet facilities; one was a coach new to British practice, an open third with central toilets, but not gangwayed. This design was later developed into a standard British Railways type. They were made up into four-coach semi-permanently coupled units and sent to the Fenchurch Street-Southend line in 1953 where they replaced some well-worn LTS and Midland coaches.

In the years between 1945 and 1949 the Southern rebuilt a number of LBSC and SEC coaches for further use on the Isle of Wight, but in this case the existing bodies were retained although some had brake compartments removed or altered. Many received steel body panels on the existing timber frames. As such, some still survive on the Isle of Wight at the time of writing—the last pre-grouping passenger stock on British Railways. The Isle of Wight stock is also the last steam-hauled stock on British Railways to retain Westinghouse brakes, although air brakes lasted on the Great Eastern section quint-arts until their withdrawal in 1960. Although by the time of the grouping in 1923 several companies had standardised the air brake, the "vacuum" companies were in the majority, and the four group companies opted for the standardisation of the vacuum system for locomotive-hauled stock. Air brakes were normally used on electric multiple-unit stock. Nevertheless, on the sections where air brakes had previously been standardised, as for example on Great Eastern lines, new stock, dual-fitted with both types of brake, had been necessary; but gradually vacuum brakes came into almost universal use in Britain with the exceptions mentioned. In the light of later

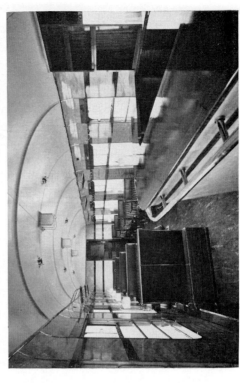

TOP RIGHT: Normal carriage lighting until recent years has been by tungsten lamps but experiments were conducted with fluorescent lighting by at least two of the group companies just before Nationalisation. Illustrated is an LMS open first. LOWER RIGHT: The interior of an LMS buffet car, one of five built in the mid-1930s.
[British Railways

developments, the decision to adopt vacuum brakes would appear to have been a mistake, and British Railways seems likely to revert to air brakes for all stock in the future.

In the matter of carriage lighting, electric lights had superseded gas during the years since the first world war, but even by the early years of Nationalisation there were still many gas-lit coaches in service—despite warnings over the years on fire danger from gas lighting. By 1955 odd gas lit coaches could still be seen on all regions except the Southern where gas had been abolished by 1939; the LMS had even built some gas-lit kitchen cars in the 1930s. (The Southern it should be noted still had a few *oil* lit horse boxes running in the 1950s!) The last gas-lit coaches, a pair of former Barry Railway brake thirds employed on the Hemyock branch of the Western Region where speeds were so low that dynamos of electrically-lit stock could not charge the batteries, did not disappear until 1961.

Tungsten light bulbs were normal on electrically-lit stock but although some experiments with fluorescent tubes were made from time to time, fluorescent lighting is only now coming into fashion on British Railways stock, although it has been standardised for some years on the more recent London Transport cars.

Soon after nationalisation, there were a number of developments in the provision of refreshment facilities on trains. Clearly the need was for an improved service of light refreshments and quick hot snacks than could be given from a normal restaurant or kitchen car which was more suited to the service of set meals. Although a few buffet cars were in existence there were not sufficient to provide the majority of trains with refreshment facilities, particularly on excursion or special trains.

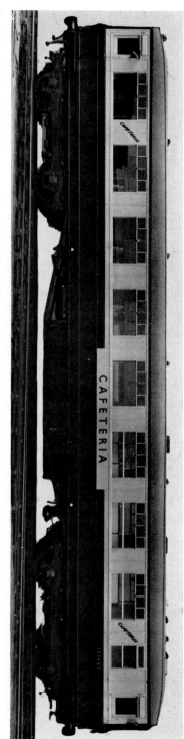

A development in railway catering services soon after Nationalisation was the introduction of cafeteria cars offering self-service meals. Most of the cars were converted from existing vehicles. Illustrated above is a former LNER coach and, below, the interior.

[British Railways

46

Many old catering vehicles were therefore converted into what became known as cafeteria cars, with help-yourself service either to your own seat or to self-contained seats in the car. Some cars had a long service counter and bar type seats so that one attendant could serve up to about 20 or so passengers from a central pantry. Although these cars did not last very long some of their ideas were later embodied in the various types of British Railways standard buffet and restaurant cars, some of which are dual-purpose vehicles serving light snacks, beverages and sandwiches from a help-yourself counter and full meals with waiter service from the kitchen to an adjoining dining saloon.

Another innovation of the early years of nationalisation was the general introduction of third class sleeping cars with two-berth compartments, each containing one lower and one upper berth provided with full bedding, a considerable improvement over the four-berth bunks then still in general use. Two-berth sleeping cars gradually replaced the four-berth type, which finally disappeared in the early 1960s. The first two-berth cars were based on pre-nationalisation designs although four years had elapsed since the old companies had vanished, but at that time British Railways standard sleeping car designs were not sufficiently advanced. Indeed, the first

British Railways sleepers did not appear until 1957 to replace the last pre-grouping and early grouping cars.

British Railways standard stock

In 1951, the first British Railways standard coaches were introduced, since when they have progressively replaced older stock and now predominate on all long-distance services. To design a coach embodying many standard features, yet capable of virtually unrestricted use throughout the British Railways system was clearly no easy task. Nevertheless, standard lengths, compartment sizes and body profile were evolved which, with few exceptions, remain the basis for present day construction. Two underframe lengths were established for bogie stock—56ft 11in and 63ft 5in. The former was used mainly for non-gangwayed suburban stock, parcels vans and full brakes, and the latter for main line corridor stock, although some suburban stock appeared on the longer underframe. A wide range of corridor designs was produced, covering both first and third class and composite side-corridor types with and without brake compartments, and first and third class open vehicles. There are several types of refreshment car from the miniature buffet—an open coach with a small bar counter—to the full kitchen car. Between are several types of restaurant car with and without buffet counters. The first full kitchens had anthracite stoves but the restaurant and buffet cars now employ Propane gas for cooking. Some of the last designs of first generation BR standard stock were various types of mail sorting and stowage vehicles for the travelling post office trains.

The non-corridor coaches were confined to brake third, third and composite types, including non-gangwayed open thirds with and without central toilet compartments. Other types of non-gangwayed stock had been envisaged, but the introduction of the modernisation programme in 1955, which provided for the development of diesel multiple-unit trains on a wide scale, and further electrification, made the locomotive-hauled non-corridor suburban coach obsolete and no new coaches of this type have been built since then.

Nevertheless, British Railways standard designs of the same basic patterns have been evolved for suburban electric services, and, in more recent years, main line corridor electric multiple-units for such services as the Southern Region's Kent Coast lines and the Eastern Region's Clacton line. Although there are variations in detail, standard dimensions have altered little. The standard side-door suburban electric coach, is based on the division of a 63ft 5in coach into ten 6ft $3\frac{1}{2}$in sections, whether they are first or third class compartments, open bays, toilets, or guards or driver's compartments. Construction with standard jigs is thus made easy. Exceptions, however, are the composite coaches on ER and LMR outer suburban sets in which the first class compartments are wider.

The British Railways standard coach designs have also introduced all-steel construction as a standard feature, with the body shell welded to the underframe to form a strong box structure. Buckeye couplers and Pullman type gangways are standard fittings on all gangwayed coaches although retractable side buffers and screw couplings are retained to allow them to be coupled to older types of stock. British Railways non-gangwayed suburban stock, however, was fitted only with side buffers and screw couplings, while electric stock couplings vary and depend on the Region for which it was built. Indeed, some electric lines have been equipped with stock which, although of British Railways standard length, is unique to a particular section; an example is the 56ft 11in suburban stock on the LMR London area services—the only British Railways electric stock on the short underframe, and the Scottish Region Glasgow open saloon stock which has air operated sliding doors and strongly resembles the LMS Southport stock.

In the field of diesel multiple-unit construction there has been far less standardisation, although standard underframe lengths have been employed. One reason is that many of the early British Railways diesel multiple-units, particularly the two-car general purpose sets, were built by outside contractors and, in consequence, several body styles and seating arrangements were employed. Diesel multiple-units are divided into three basic patterns: non-gangwayed suburban units of three or four-car sets, all of which are of the open pattern with side doors to each seating bay, some coaches are fitted with toilets and some include first class accommodation. Second are the general purpose units which may be used on suburban, cross-country or main-line services. Most are in two-car units but there are some three- and four-car units; all contain toilets and first class accommodation and are usually gangwayed within the set except on the Southern Region diesel-electric units. Finally, there are the express units for inter-city services, which are similar to locomotive-hauled coaches; they include both open and side corridor accommodation, are gangwayed through the set and some include buffet cars. A feature of many diesel units is the observation view given to passengers at the front and back through the driver's cabs.

Some of the diesel units are of lightweight construction but most are steel bodied. In fact, the weight of ordinary British Railways steel stock has gradually risen as such new features as double-glazed windows and other improved passenger amenities have been introduced, and, particularly, by heavier bogies, which raised the weight of an ordinary corridor second, for example, to 37 tons. Train weights were thus being increased without any increase in carrying capacity, a serious matter where overall train weights were made critical by the more precise performance of diesel locomotives.

One feature of the earlier British Railways standard coaches which did not prove successful was bogies. The original British Railways standard bogie, which was produced in two versions—a double-bolster type for locomotive-hauled stock and a single bolster type for electric multiple-units, together with a similar type for diesel multiple-units—was based on selected features of the bogies of the four group companies. While the bogie gave a good ride when freshly overhauled,

performance soon deteriorated to give rough riding, particularly on welded track. In an endeavour to find a solution and to provide a bogie which would give a good ride even at the 100 m.p.h. speeds promised for the future, British Railways engineers started afresh with a simple design similar to the latest Swiss and German bogies, employing coil springs on both primary and secondary suspension, in contrast to the leaf springs almost traditional since the beginning of railways. While the new bogie was being developed, many new British Railways coaches were mounted on Commonwealth bogies.

In 1956 the European Railway Union finally abolished three-class travel on most European Railways, which meant that there was no longer any need for three classes on British Railways Continental boat trains. From June 3, 1956, therefore, the existing second class was abolished and third class was renamed second class. In effect it was third class which disappeared, 112 years after Gladstone's 1844 Act, had reached the statute book.

At the present time British Railways engineers are experimenting with coaches of integral design in which the body is self-supporting; shorn of a heavy independent underframe the weight has been brought down to about 30 tons, but since the coach is of normal steel construction it is still heavier than much longer Continental coaches of 78-87ft which are of lightweight steel and aluminium construction, weigh no more than about 25-28 tons and carry 80-96 passengers. Apart from isolated examples of lightweight construction on British main line railways, as for example the LMS 1938 Liverpool-Southport electric stock, or an experimental coach built by the Western Region in about 1949, the general use of lightweight stock has been confined to London Transport. As we have already seen, London Transport coach design has been fairly standardised since 1938 with two basic types of stock, one for the sub-surface Metropolitan and District lines, and a smaller version for the deep level tube lines. From about 1950 London Transport introduced aluminium-bodied vehicles to its District line and since about 1956 similar tube stock cars were developed and placed in service on the Central and Piccadilly lines.

For the re-equipment of the Metropolitan Amersham and Uxbridge lines from 1960, London Transport developed another design of open stock more suited to the outer suburban character of the services. The new stock was also of lightweight aluminium construction but although built for sub-surface lines in the inner London area, at one time subject to loading gauge restrictions which barred the passage of stock larger than the normal Metropolitan 54ft 6in coaches, it is currently the widest stock in the country, 9ft 8in wide over the body panels. The added inches allow comfortable three- and two-seating inside compared with the cramped British Railways three- and two-seating in stock 8in narrower.

Some of the tight clearances still exist in the tunnels between Finchley Road and Baker Street which has meant that the Metropolitan 1960 stock slopes inwards from waist to roof level to give sufficient clearance. Some sections of line with tight clearances demanding rolling stock restrictions or prohibitions are well-known even to the extent of being branded on some Continental train-ferry freight wagons—"Not to work on the Metropolitan Railway between Finchley Road and Baker Street or on the Southern Railway between Tonbridge and Battle or Canterbury and Whitstable".

The future

The traditional British coach has now virtually reached the limit of development and future improvements are likely to be in the field of decor, heating, lighting, new materials and in standards of passenger comfort. Electric heating, for many years used on electric multiple-units, is becoming standard for locomotive hauled stock on electrified lines, and may even be adopted where diesel-electric traction is used, thus removing the last link with the steam locomotive—steam heating—for which diesel and early d.c. electric locomotives had to be

equipped with small boilers. Ease of construction and maintenance will play a big part in design, and carriage interiors may well be built up from pre-fabricated plastic components. Indeed, experiments are now in hand with plastic coach bodies, and bodies built to aircraft principals, which, if successful, could result in considerable weight saving and maintenance costs. Full air-conditioning will be used on luxury stock and pressure ventilation on ordinary main line stock. Although the Pullman Car Company, which operated Pullman cars on selected services has been merged into the British Railways organisation, Pullmans, offering luxury accommodation will be included in many expresses of the future on all parts of British Railways. It seems likely that in future there will be two or possibly three standards of accommodation, ordinary, first class and Pullman, the latter providing a superior type of first class accommodation with more luxurious appointments and with more personal service for meals and refreshments.

Already British Railways have new trains embodying some of these principles, for example, the diesel multiple-unit Blue Pullmans on the Western and, until recently, the LMR air conditioned throughout and with partly reclining seats in the first class saloons, and the new locomotive-hauled Pullmans on the Eastern Region and on the new electric expresses between Euston, Liverpool and Manchester. The XP64 "Train of Tomorrow" prototype train is at present on trial with many new constructional features and experimental decor. Most notable are the wider doors, and large entrance vestibules spaced more evenly along the carriage side, which will be of convenience to passengers carrying luggage. New liveries are under examination and all new stock is likely to be fitted with air brakes which have been proved over many years to be more powerful and quicker acting than vacuum brakes. Disc brakes will make for smoother deceleration.

The train of the future is an exciting prospect; higher speeds, smooth riding and improved passenger amenities will make it equal if not superior to other space age transport.

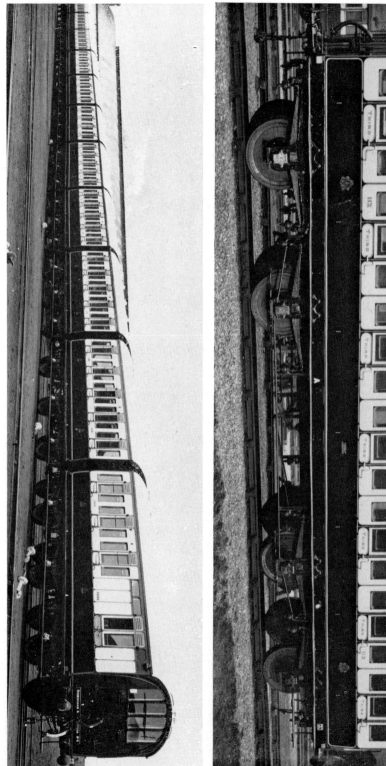

LNWR.
Non-corridor stock
1880-1911

Until the early 1880s LNW coaches were four or six wheelers with a maximum length of 33ft. In 1883 the LNW introduced longer, 42ft vehicles carried on a radial eight-wheel underframe in which the centre axles were mounted in fixed axleboxes and the outer axles in separate trucks with radial side-play. Illustrated TOP LEFT is a full third of this pattern. By about 1906, when non-corridor stock was becoming confined to suburban and shorter distance main-line services, LNW stock was 50ft or more in length with a low elliptical roof, typified by the 50ft lavatory first (RIGHT and BELOW) employed on Euston-Rugby services. Yet non-bogie coaches were still being built for some suburban services; illustrated LEFT BELOW is the 11-coach set of six-wheelers built in 1911 for the Birmingham and Sutton service.

[British Railways

LNWR
Corridor stock 1900-1908

The first LNW stock with through gangways, placed in service in 1893 on the afternoon Euston-Glasgow/Edinburgh trains, was little different in size from non-corridor LNW coaches of the period—short, low arc-roofed vehicles of 42ft in length and 8ft wide. By the end of the 19th century the radial eight wheel arrangement had given place to bogies, and coaches were 50ft long: by the early years of the present century 57ft had become the standard length for LNW stock. The roof profile too, developed from the low arc roof of the corridor composite (TOP LEFT) built about 1900 and seen here after it had been transferred to the Midland & Great

Northern Joint line 1937, to the flattened elliptical roof of the brake tri-composite BELOW LEFT, and the high elliptical roof of the tri-composite ABOVE. The brake tri-composite (LEFT) had two third class compartments, one second, two firsts, and a centre guard's compartment and was employed on through services between Euston, Llandrindod Wells and the LNW Central Wales line. The tri-composite ABOVE is representative of standard LNW stock from 1908 until 1923—57ft long and 9ft wide over body. On the RIGHT is the interior of the same coach.

[H. C. Casserley; British Railways

53

LNWR
Special sets and diners 1907-10

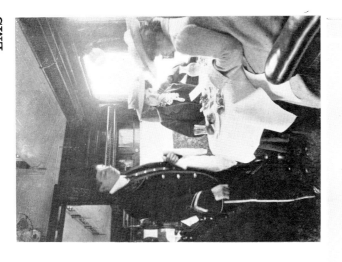

In 1907 and 1908 the LNW introduced on its Liverpool-London American boat trains and afternoon London-Scottish services respectively some ordinary coaches of the same general dimensions and styling as its magnificent twelve-wheel diners and sleepers, but with elliptical roofs. The American boat train was of uniform profile throughout, unusual in LNW practice, and included two 50ft eight-wheel full brakes and a kitchen car. The passenger coaches consisted of two firsts, a first diner, a second and third class diner, and a second and third class corridor coach. The first class coaches included some extra large compartments with sofas and armchairs.

The 1908 Anglo-Scottish trains included earlier clerestory diners in the formation, and the compartments were of normal dimensions. Illustrated FAR LEFT is a first class compartment of the 1908 West Coast Joint Stock; NEARER LEFT is a large first class compartment of the American boat train and, BELOW LEFT, the second and third class composite of the American boat train. RIGHT is the interior of an LNW diner of about 1900 and, BELOW, the dining car of the short-lived Birmingham New Street-London Broad Street service, typical of LNW diners built after 1908.

[British Railways]

LNWR
Saloons

The first of the saloons illustrated, LEFT, is that which belonged to the Duke of Sutherland and was not owned by the LNW although it was built by the LNWR at Wolverton in 1900 and anticipated in many respects a number of LNW saloons built in the following years. It was liveried in an almost black dark green and off-white instead of LNW purple-brown and spilt milk. Accommodation included a general day saloon, sleeping compartments and a small kitchen. BELOW is one of the LNW 57ft saloons, built in the first years of the present century, which, although described as family carriages and could be

hired by the wealthy, were more usually found as part of the LNW Royal train, for they matched in contour the two Royal saloons built by the LNW in 1903 (illustrated on page 27). Internally these saloons had day and night accommodation. Similar in many respects to family saloons were invalid saloons, but as their name implies they were designed specially for the conveyance of invalids and included a bed and special accommodation for a nurse. Illustrated RIGHT and BELOW is an LNW invalid saloon, seen in LMS livery.

[G. M. Kichenside; British Railways

LNWR and Midland Sleepers

From the introduction of the 65ft 6in clerestory 12-wheel sleeping car in the late-1890s, developments took the form of the suppression of the clerestory a decade later, and the gradual widening of the entrance vestibules, until, by the 1920s, the last LNW sleepers had almost full

width entrance vestibules (LEFT UPPER). But the last LNW-pattern sleeping cars did not appear until 1928 when the LMS built two cars of basically LNW design (LEFT LOWER) with detail modifications for the St. Pancras-Edinburgh service operated by Midland & North British Joint cars. The Midland itself had employed Pullman sleepers for many years and even in 1900 had placed in service new cars of partly open pattern internally, built by Pullman in America and assembled at Derby (BELOW) but by 1906 was building sleeping cars of normal Midland clerestory roof type, 65ft long, with standard transverse berths (RIGHT).

[British Railways

Midland and LTS stock 1880-1915

The Midland was one of the first companies to introduce bogie stock in the mid-1870s, but continued to build non-bogie stock until the 1890s. Illustrated BELOW is a Midland main line bogie third of the 1880s and, LEFT, a suburban four-wheel third as used on the Moorgate service at the turn of the century. Notice the two gas lamps to each compartment. Although Clayton introduced coaches of a massive clerestory

pattern in 1896 (illustrated on page 24) the suburban stock introduced by David Bain from about 1910 was not unlike Clayton's stock of 1880. RIGHT is a Bain lavatory composite, part of a 13-coach set of wide-body stock built for the London, Tilbury & Southend line in 1915. BELOW is a standard LTS bogie composite of the period 1900-11, but similar to earlier LTS non-bogie carriages.
[British Railways; G. M. Kichenside

Midland Diners 1893-1906

Following the introduction of dining cars in 1893 the Midland became noted for the excellence of its train catering. But it was not until several years later that corridors were provided through the whole way in the diner or had to passengers taking meals travelled the whole way in the diner or had to change carriages at an intermediate stop. The first Midland diners were formed from pairs of vehicles, one first and the other third class, with kitchen and pantry accommodation, and with both vehicles gang-wayed together at their adjoining ends. The first class cars were

62

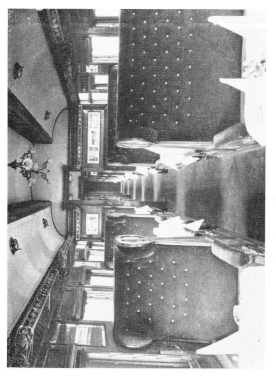

spacious, with every passenger occupying a single armchair seat. Third-class cars had an additional seating bay and three-a-side seating. Illustrated, LEFT and BELOW LEFT, is a first class car built in about 1893 for the Midland & Glasgow & South Western Joint service. Clayton's massive 65ft clerestory diners were similar to his ordinary stock of the 1896-1904 period; they introduced the two windows per seating bay arrangement, a feature of Midland and LMS open stock for many years; illustrated RIGHT and BELOW is an M&GSW first class diner of 1904.

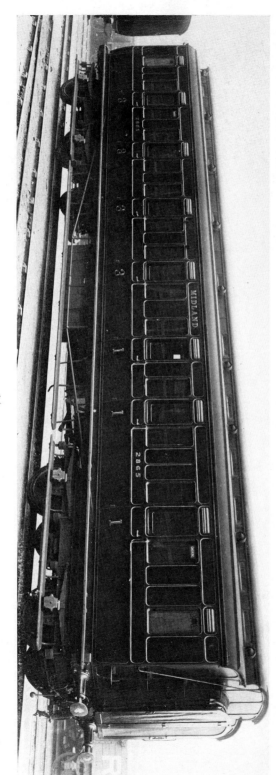

64

Midland Corridor stock 1905-22

The Midland was one of the first companies to employ the clerestory roof for coaching stock in the 1870s but abandoned it within a few years; in 1896 Clayton introduced a more massive clerestory in which the coach ends continued unbroken into the upper deck, a pattern employed with only slight alteration until the Midland adopted

the high elliptical roof from about 1918. Illustrated LEFT is a 50ft semi-open third containing at the far end a saloon with longitudinal seats, one of a number of coaches of this type which were allocated to the Midland & Great Northern Joint line. LEFT BELOW is a 54ft corridor composite of about 1910; RIGHT, is a 54ft brake composite and BELOW a 60ft third class diner built for the St. Pancras-Glasgow service in the early 1920s.

[British Railways

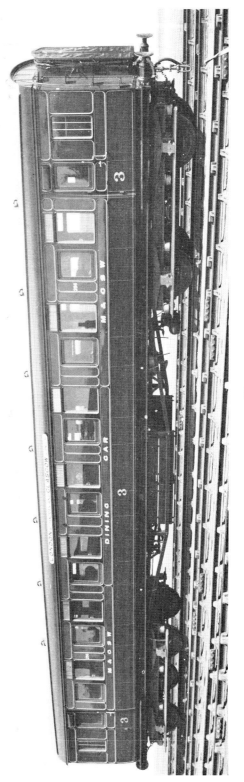

Corridor stock—
Highland
Caledonian

Of the other LMS constituent companies the Caledonian and Lancashire & Yorkshire made extensive use of corridor stock from the turn of the century. In 1905/6 the Caledonian produced some magnificent 65ft 12-wheelers for its Glasgow/Edinburgh-Aberdeen "Grampian" service; BELOW is a Grampian composite. RIGHT LOWER is a Lancashire & Yorkshire open composite, part of a set train of "fireproof" gas lit centre corridor stock built in 1914. The Highland had coaches with through gangways but relied to a great extent on non-gangwayed vehicles with internal corridors or between-compartment toilets; LEFT is a semi-corridor composite. RIGHT UPPER is a Furness 49ft composite, one of two built in 1906.

[Iain Smith, British Railways

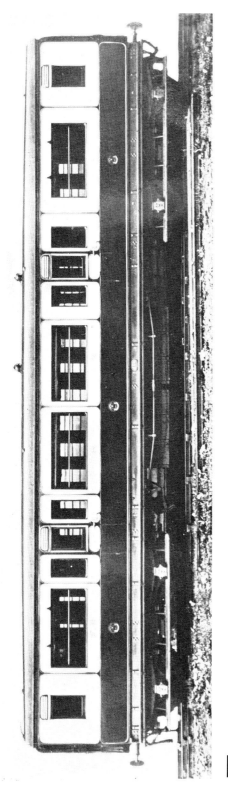

Furness

Lancashire & Yorkshire

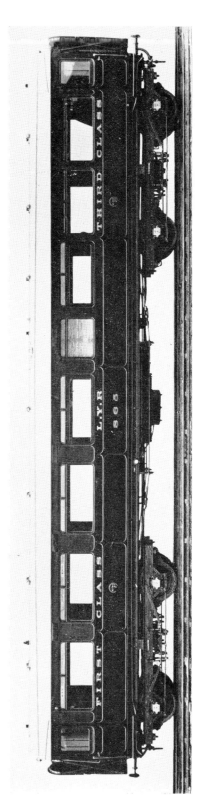

LTSR
Ealing-Southend
corridor train 1911

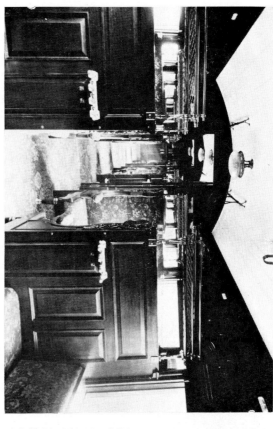

The standard London, Tilbury & Southend coach, illustrated on page 61, was normally employed on the principal trains between Southend and Fenchurch Street. Some coaches had between-compartment toilets but corridor stock was not normally used by the LTSR, except on the through trains between Ealing and Southend. These coaches had through gangways and were of the open pattern internally. The brake thirds alone had toilet facilities, which incorporated cess tanks beneath the coaches to prevent the discharge of effluence on the underground sections of the District Railway. BELOW is a complete train and, LEFT, the interior of the composite.

[British Railways

NLR and
S&D stock

Of the smaller LMS constituents, the North London relied exclusively on close-coupled sets of four-wheelers for its entire existence (RIGHT). These austere trains were a familiar sight in North and East London until the mid-1930s. The second major joint line in which the Midland was involved was the Somerset & Dorset, jointly owned with the LSWR. The S&D brake third, BELOW, shows affinities to practices of both Derby and Eastleigh.

[H. C. Casserley; British Railways

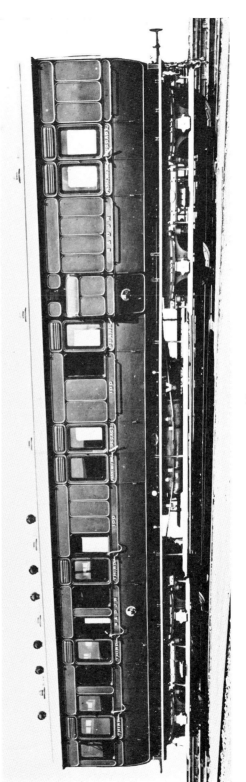

Railmotors—
LNW, Furness, GSW

During the first decade of the present century many railways developed light rail motor units for operation on branches and on lightly used main line stopping services. The railmotors themselves consisted of a carriage with a steam engine unit either mounted on a bogie within the coach body as in the LNW unit illustrated on this page, or as an outside locomotive portion to which the coach was attached by an articulated coupling like the Glasgow & South Western unit, RIGHT LOWER. The Furness unit, TOP RIGHT, was designed to work with a four-wheel trailer coach. Lack of reserve power to handle extra traffic soon caused the railmotor to go out of favour.

[British Railways

70

Observation and Club saloons

The coach TOP LEFT started life as an LNW 42ft picnic saloon in 1896, a vehicle which could be hired by parties for day trips. In 1922 it was converted for use as a club saloon by business men's travelling clubs on residential trains between Manchester and Lancashire and North Wales Coast towns—a mode of travel fostered by the LNW and L&Y. Only club members were allowed to travel in the coach and strict rules governed club members in such things as seat allocations, and the opening of windows, etc. This traffic was sufficiently lucrative for the LMS to build a new 60ft saloon in 1935 for the Manchester-Blackpool club train. (RIGHT and BELOW). FACING PAGE LOWER is an LNW observation saloon built in about 1911 for the Blaeau Ffestiniog branch. It has since been preserved by the Bluebell Railway.
[British Railways

74

LMS 1928
Semi-open first

A coach which made its debut in "The Royal Scot" and other LMS services in 1928 was a 57ft semi-open first, with three side-corridor compartments each seating only four passengers (thus everyone had a corner seat), a central toilet, and a three bay, three-a-side open saloon, usually run next to a kitchen car and used for dining purposes. Only 16 vehicles of this type were built, between 1928 and 1932; the first batch (illustrated below) had panelled bodies with a high waistline, but the following batch had deep windows without the waist panelling. The last vehicle was of the steel-sided pattern.

[British Railways

LMS " Royal Scot "
lounge brake

Another coach introduced with " The Royal Scot ", but in this instance unique to this service, was a 57ft first class lounge brake. Passenger accommodation consisted of a single saloon occupying about half the coach and containing eight arm chairs with fixed semi-circular tables between them. First class passengers could thus use the lounge for short periods as an alternative to their own seat in one of the compartments. A feature of this and other LMS corridor and open coaches of this period was the rotating glass vane ventilator above the large saloon windows.
[British Railways

75

LMS Corridor stock 1930

From about 1929 the large windows in LMS corridor and open coaches were made deeper with the result that the waist panel was eliminated. This style was employed between 1929 and 1932 but only a few side corridor vehicles of this pattern were built. Illustrated BELOW and LEFT is a corridor third, unusual because it was 60ft long compared with the normal length of 57ft for LMS thirds. Large quantities of open thirds of this pattern, mostly 57ft long, but some 60ft, of wood-panelled and steel-sided types appeared at this time. Large drop windows were provided in compartments and some bays. The passengers in this view will not be travelling far—it was a posed shot in the North London bay at Willesden Junction!

[British Railways

76

LMS Corridor stock 1933-39

From the end of 1932 when Stanier became chief mechanical engineer LMS carriage design underwent a further change. Although timber body framing was still used, steel panels formed the outer skin of sides, ends and roof. All protrusions such as window frames were eliminated. The cumbersome drop window and rotating glass ventilators were replaced by fixed windows and sliding window ventilators, features which are still standard on the latest BR stock. Illustrated RIGHT and BELOW is an open third; similar designs were evolved for side corridor stock, of both first and third class, and brake vehicles.

[British Railways

LMS Non-Corridor stock 1923-47

R. W. Reid the LMS carriage superintendent standardised two lengths for LMS non-corridor stock—54ft and 57ft, the former usually employed for stock destined for lines already operating 54ft stock. Like corridor stock, LMS non-corridor stock went through the design change from wooden-panelled bodies to timber-framed steel flush-sided bodies between 1927 and 1933. Some coaches had between-compartment toilets, like the 57ft lavatory brake third illustrated

BELOW. TOP RIGHT is a five coach set train—brake third, composite, first, composite, brake third—built in 1926 for the Cathcart Circle service in Glasgow. Three of the coaches were 54ft long but the two composites were only 51ft, the shortest LMS passenger vehicles ever built. RIGHT LOWER is a steel flush-sided 57ft composite of the mid-1930s, with a simplified version of the full lining.

[British Railways

LMS Dining cars

The LMS provided extensive catering facilities on many long distance expresses; where a large number of meals were required a full kitchen car (LEFT) would be employed with open coaches. A smaller demand would be met by a kitchen first (or third) coupled to a single open vehicle. Nearly all LMS full kitchen cars were equipped for gas cooking and lighting. All LMS-built restaurant cars with kitchens were 12-wheelers.
[British Railways

LMS 1941
Royal saloons

In 1941 the LMS built two new 12-wheel Royal saloons 69ft long by 9ft wide, respectively the King's and Queen's saloons, to replace the two principal saloons built in 1903 for the LNWR Royal train (illustrated on page 27). Both were equipped for day and night travel with lounges, bedroom, dressing and bathrooms, also accommodation for personal staff. A number of features were unusual in LMS carriage practice, among them double-glazed windows, full air conditioning and the provision of buck-eye couplers and Pullman-type gangways. Shutters were fitted over the windows as a wartime precaution and have since been removed. Both coaches were heavy by normal standards, taring 57 tons. Illustrated right and below is the Queen's saloon. A power car was built at the same time, and, subsequently BR has added a dining car and two other saloons for the present royal train.

[British Railways

LMS
Sleeping cars

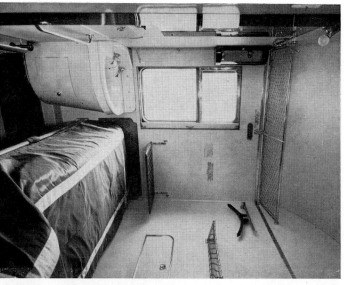

As we have already seen, the first sleeping cars built by the LMS were basically of LNW pattern but 68ft in length; indeed 51 LNW-type first class cars were built between 1924 and 1930. The first purely LMS designs were the 60ft third class sleepers built in 1928 in readiness for the introduction of third class sleeping facilities in that year. Each of the seven compartments contained four berths, two lower and two upper, provided only with a rug and pillow. There were no external doors to the compartments and each had a centre droplight flanked by quarterlights. Entry to the coach was by end doors. Below is one of the later cars of this type

built in 1931 with steel body panels. The interior is illustrated on page 37. In 1930 came the first LMS composite sleepers (TOP RIGHT) 65ft long in which the four third class compartments had droplights and quarter lights, like the all-third cars, and deep single windows similar to those in the LNW pattern cars in each first class compartment. RIGHT LOWER is a later LMS composite sleeper built in 1936, 69ft long with six first class and four third class compartments. BELOW LEFT is the interior of a first class sleeping compartment. With the exception of the all-third class cars, all LMS sleepers were 12-wheelers.

[British Railways

LMS "Coronation Scot" 1937-39

In 1937 both the LMS and LNER introduced new high speed express trains between London and Scotland, the former the "Coronation Scot", the latter the "Coronation". As we shall see later, the LNER placed in service new set trains for its "Coronation" service; the LMS also produced nominally new sets for the "Coronation Scot", three trains in fact, two for service and one spare. The trains certainly carried new livery, blue with silver stripes, but most of the coaches had been converted from existing ordinary LMS stock. First class compartments had

two-a-side seating, and pressure ventilation was employed. Third class seating, and seats in open saloons of both classes were three-a-side. Illustrated left is the interior of an open third and left lower is the nine-coach train which included two full kitchen cars. The LMS authorities soon realised that their "Coronation Scot" trains did not match those of the rival LNER "Coronation" and were soon planning new sets for introduction in 1940. Part-integral construction, articulation of coaches in pairs, and such gimmicks as telephones in each compartment to the dining cars and a lounge car were planned for the new trains. Part of one of the new trains, including sleeping and club cars, was sent on a tour of the USA in 1939 but war broke out and the train remained in the USA until 1946; although three new sets were completed after the war the service was not restored. Illustrated right is one of the 1939 train dining saloons and below the American tour train.   [British Railways

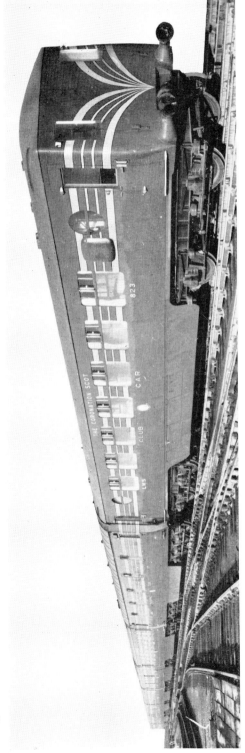

NS and GKE
Light and narrow
gauge

Among the minor railways taken over by the LMS at grouping were the Leek & Manifold Valley Light Railway, a nominally independent 2ft 6in gauge line, but worked by the North Staffordshire Railway, and the standard gauge Garstang & Knott End Railway. Both had unique types of coach unlike normal British stock. BELOW is a Garstang & Knott End third class open coach with end balconies. LEFT are two of the Leek & Manifold's four coaches, a full third and brake composite. Both were 42ft long and 8ft wide—despite the narrow gauge; the thirds seated 44 passengers and weighed about 12½ tons and the brake composites seated eight first and 22 third class passengers and weighed nearly 13 tons.

[H. C. Casserley

LMS
Diesel train 1938

Following its earlier unsuccessful diesel train experiment in 1928, the LMS introduced a new three-car articulated diesel train in 1938 which, after trials on the St. Pancras-Bedford service, was employed on the Oxford-Bletchley-Cambridge line. The two end cars were 63ft 9¾in long and the centre car 51ft 9in long over underframes. The train seated 24 first and 138 third class passengers in open saloon accommodation and the seat backs were reversible to allow passengers to face in either direction. Air operated sliding doors were under the control of the guard and the unit was powered by six Leyland 125hp engines with hydraulic transmission. RIGHT is a third class saloon and BELOW the complete unit.

[British Railways]

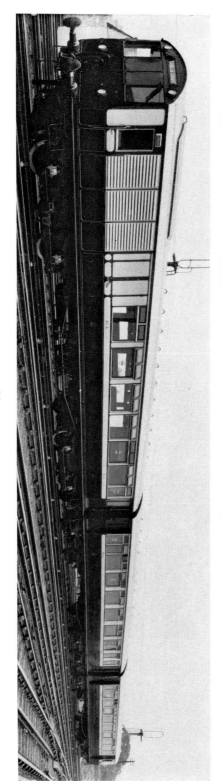

LNWR and LMS Electric stock

For its London suburban electrification programme begun in 1914 with the conversion of the Willesden-Earls Court line and completed in 1922 when electric trains reached Euston, the LNW adopted 57ft open saloon pattern vehicles in three-car sets, with gangways between coaches within the set but not at the driving ends. The first four sets, with Siemens electrical equipment, for the Willesden-Earls Court service, differed in detail from the later sets, which had Oerlikon equipment, for the remainder of the LNW electrification scheme. Right is a Siemens motor brake third of 1914; with pantographs and new a.c. equipment they spent their last years on the Lancaster, Morecambe & Heysham line. LEFT LOWER is a three-car Oerlikon set, with, above, the interiors of Oerlikon first class and third class saloons. Below is an LMS three-car compartment set of 1927 with 59ft motor coach and 57ft trailers; some of these units retained the elaborate "panelled" lining at least until 1947.

[British Railways

L&Y electric Liverpool-Southport

In 1904 the L&Y electrified its Liverpool-Southport line, for which it built some of the widest stock ever to operate outside the Great Western broad gauge lines. The L&Y Southport electric stock was 60ft long, and 9ft 10⅜in wide over body panels. The open saloon pattern was adopted with entry through end swing doors and the coaches had straight sides and clerestory roofs. A considerable amount of metal was used in construction including aluminium for fittings and panelling. Illustrated LEFT is the interior and BELOW the exterior of a first class car.

[British Railways

LMS electric Liverpool-Southport

When the L&Y Southport stock became life-expired in the late 1930s the LMS introduced new sets of lightweight stock of integral construction, which, despite their size—66ft 6in long and 9ft 3in wide over body panels, were among the lightest standard gauge electric coaches of main line dimensions with comparable equipment, 41tons for the motor coaches and 24tons for the trailers. Like their L&Y predecessors, third class saloon seating was five-a-side and first class four-a-side. Air-operated sliding doors were under the control of the guard. RIGHT is the interior of a third class saloon, and BELOW is a three-car train.
[British Railways

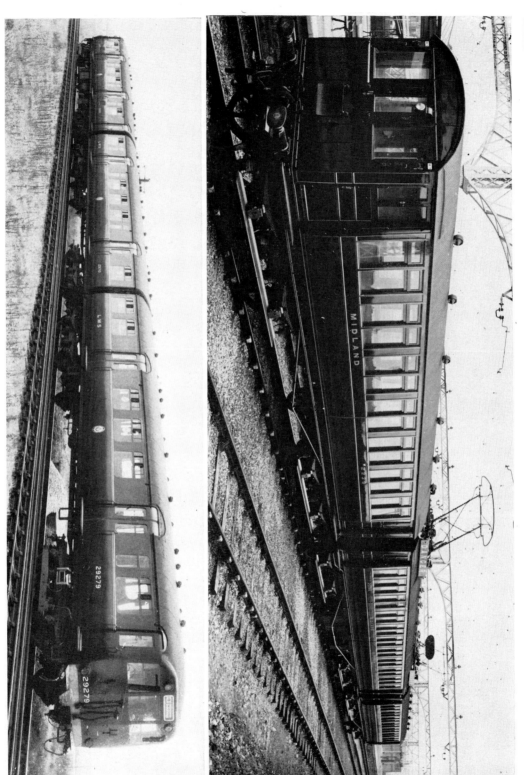

LMS, Midland and L&Y Electric stock

The Midland Railway did not go in for electrification on a big scale and confined itself to the more-or-less self contained area between Lancaster, Morecambe and Heysham, which it converted in 1908 on the 6,600V a.c. overhead system. Three 60ft motor coaches and four 43ft driving trailers were built specially for the line, and one or two other coaches were converted from steam stock. TOP LEFT is a three car train of the LM&H line. BELOW LEFT is a three-car set of LMS Wirral stock built in 1938 for the Liverpool Central (Low Level)-West Kirby service which ran over the Mersey Railway. This stock, of lightweight construction, was similar though smaller than the LMS Southport stock of the following year. RIGHT is a motor brake third built in 1915 for the L&Y Manchester-Bury line. It was similar in many respects to the earlier L&Y Southport stock and was of all-metal construction. BELOW is a 58ft compartment motor brake third weighing 57tons built in 1931 for the Manchester-Altrincham line, then jointly-owned by the LNER and LMS, but now included in the LMR.

[British Railways]

TPO vehicles

An early feature of railway working was the conveyance and sorting of mail in special mail carriages; by 1838, equipment had been developed which allowed mail bags to be picked up by, and set down from trains travelling at speed. Since then, basic mail exchange apparatus has changed little, but mail coaches have developed in line with other types of railway carriage. Below is a London & North Western 50ft sorting carriage with exchange apparatus, built soon after the turn of the century. Left is the interior of the same vehicle. Top right is a Midland clerestory TPO coach seen here on the Newcastle-Bristol service, jointly worked by the LMS and LNER with Midland and North Eastern Joint postal stock. Below right is a standard LMS 60ft TPO coach of the mid-1930s.

[British Railways; H. C. Casserley

GNR 1900-1911

The Great Northern made extensive use of four-wheel stock on its London suburban services, long after other London companies had adopted bogie vehicles for similar services in other parts of the capital. Most were short coaches, no more than 8ft wide, but, in 1900, the GN placed in service some wide-body four-wheelers seating six-a-side in the third class compartments in the same manner as on the GE wide-body stock of a year or so earlier. Because of loading gauge limits doors were recessed. Some of these four-wheelers were long lived; indeed some survived until the mid-1930s on some of the branches in North London. On the left is a wide-body

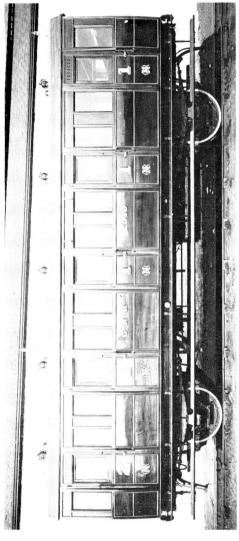

brake third of 1900, and on the right a first/second composite of the same stock. In 1911 Gresley introduced new stock for London suburban services, eight coach trains of articulated twins. Soon after, the well-known articulated four-coach sets, the "quad arts", normally working in pairs as eight-coach trains, made their appearance. One set of each train was third class; the other included first and second class. Because of overall length restrictions, the brake and adjacent coach of each quad-set were shorter than the other two vehicles. Illustrated below is a third class quad-art. Gas lighting was employed.

[British Railways

London suburban

East Coast stock
1896-1922

The East Coast route was not one on which bogie coaches made an early appearance. Six-wheelers and non-bogie eight wheelers remained on East Coast express services until the mid-1890s. The typical East Coast and GN main line coach was a short, narrow vehicle, with a low elliptical roof, almost flat on top. Illustrated LEFT is a lavatory composite built in the 1890s. BELOW is a 55ft ECJS corridor third of the late 1890s with clerestory roof, and end and side doors. This particular coach has been preserved by the BRB and is at present stored. TOP RIGHT is the final type of GN and ECJS coach, with high elliptical roof, domed at the ends. This particular vehicle is a brake third. BELOW RIGHT is a North Eastern Railway corridor third, similar in general appearance to Gresley's GN stock but with rounded windows and panelling.

[T. J. Edgington; British Railways; G. M. Kichenside

East Coast dining cars 1900-1922

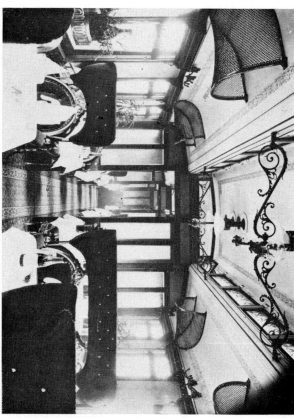

The Great Northern took the lead in the provision of dining facilities with the introduction of a Pullman dining car between Kings Cross and Leeds in 1879. In 1893, in common with the Midland and the LNW, third class dining facilities appeared on East Coast trains with a six-wheel kitchen car flanked by first and third class dining bogie saloons. By the turn of the century, bogie vehicles, usually 12-wheelers, were employed on East Coast expresses. BELOW is a composite dining car, with a central kitchen, of the late 1890s, and left is the interior of a first class car. In 1906 Gresley abandoned the clerestory roof on some new four-coach trains for the Kings Cross-Sheffield service, which included a 12-wheel composite diner, RIGHT UPPER. GN and ECJS carriages of this period set the

pattern of coaching stock in Eastern England for the next 35 years. In 1921 Gresley built a five-coach articulated train for the Kings Cross–Leeds service (BELOW), which included a full kitchen, and first and third class dining saloons. The kitchen car employed electricity for cooking, obtained from batteries charged by the train dynamos—the first appearance of the all-electric kitchen in train catering, later standardised on LNER restaurant cars.

[British Railways

GE Suburban stock 1899-1910

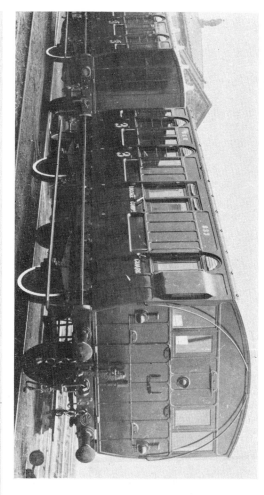

To increase the carrying capacity of Great Eastern suburban trains, James Holden introduced in 1899 a new train of four-wheel suburban coaches with 9ft instead of 8ft-wide bodies, seating 12 passengers in each third class compartment. LEFT is one of the brake thirds. The train was such a success that Holden performed a widening operation on earlier 8ft wide coaches to bring them to the same standards. (See page 24.) Later many of the four-wheelers were rebuilt in pairs on bogie underframes (BELOW).

[British Railways

GE Six-wheel main-line stock

The Great Eastern was one of the last of the major companies to adopt bogie stock; indeed the first did not appear until 1897 and large numbers of six-wheel coaches both with and without lavatories were built until the turn of the century. Mixed with bogie stock, six-wheelers continued in use for several years on GE expresses. Some were long lived; the last, on the Haughley-Laxfield branch, were withdrawn in 1949. RIGHT is lavatory third and, BELOW, the Laxfield branch train composed of two lavatory composites and a brake third.

[H. C. Casserley; T. J. Edgington

GE
Main line stock
1904-8

Even when the Great Eastern built a corridor train, gangwayed throughout, for the Hook of Holland boat service in 1904, it included three six-wheel coaches—two brake vans and a two compartment corridor brake second. All the bogie vehicles had clerestory roofs and recessed round-top doors. The complete train is seen BELOW and the brake second in close up, LEFT. The Great Eastern's first bogie coaches built in 1897 were semi-corridor composites, 48ft 3in long over underframes, with clerestory roofs. (BELOW). By 1908, elliptical-roofed bogie stock, usually 50ft long, had become the future GE standard. Illustrated ABOVE is a corridor third.

[H. C. Casserley; L.P.C.

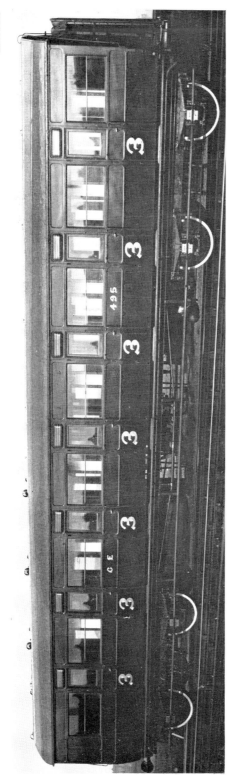

GE Dining set 1891

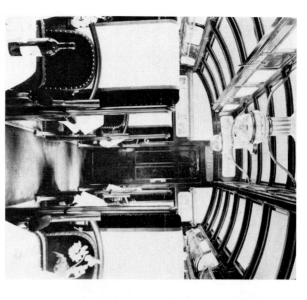

The Great Eastern led the way in the introduction of third class dining facilities, which were included in a six-wheel three-coach dining set built in 1891 for the Harwich-North of England Continental boat service. The three vehicles were connected by side gangways but the set was not gangwayed at the outer ends. The centre coach was the dining car, 34ft 6in long, 9ft wide over the passenger saloon and 6in less at the coach ends. The vehicle nearer the camera was a first

and second class composite, with two compartments of each class and two toilets, all linked by side corridor The coach on the far side of the diner was a full third with four compartments linked to toilet facilities and to the diner, but with one compartment at the far end cut off from the rest of the coach. The set is seen below marshalled with two brake vans and bearing roofboards "York Antwerp Rotterdam Hamburg via Harwich". Left is the interior of the dining saloon.

M&GN composite Wisbech & Upwell coach

Among some of the more unusual coaches taken over by the LNER was the tramway type coach with end balconies, built originally for the Wisbech & Upwell tramway. The coach was later transferred to the Kelvedon & Tollesbury light railway, which needed stock with ground level access because of the low platforms. In 1952 the coach was used for filming in the "Titfield Thunderbolt" following which it was restored for preservation but broken up for lack of storage space. It is seen BELOW as restored. On the RIGHT is a Midland & Great Northern six-wheel composite inherited by the M&GN from the Eastern & Midlands Railway.

[H. C. Casserley; R. C. Riley

NER Non-corridor stock 1895-1912

The carriage superintendent of the North Eastern at the turn of the century was David Bain, later of the Midland Railway. NER coaches built during the 1890s and the early years of the present century were gas-lit and usually had clerestory roofs. Some had toilet facilities with internal part corridors. BELOW is a late-1890s brake third. Later coaches had high elliptical roofs, although gas lighting was retained for some years. LEFT is a full third of the later pattern. For a year or two early in the present century the NER introduced a new design of stock with straight, matchboarded sides, windows with toplights, gas lighting and elliptical roofs. RIGHT is a semi-corridor lavatory third of this pattern.

[G. M. Kichenside; L.P.C.; H. C. Casserley

GNS
Non corridor stock

The Great North of Scotland, one of the smallest of the major constituents of the LNER at Grouping, had some neat coaching stock designs with some distinguishing features, among them toplights above the windows, the bulbous ventilator hoods in the doors and the style of body panelling. The Great North did not have a large number of corridor coaches and much of its traffic was local in character. RIGHT is a non-corridor third.

[T. J. Edgington]

Great Central suburban

The Great Central was the last railway to reach London and the London suburban services generally had the benefit of new stock from the start. From the turn of the century the GC placed in service some handsome non-gangwayed stock with clerestory roofs. BELOW is a 50ft, eight-compartment full third. In 1912 the Great Central conducted experiments in the Manchester and London areas with a petrol-electric railcar, seen LEFT running with a Manchester, Sheffield & Lincolnshire six-wheel composite.
[H. Gordon Tidey; British Railways

110

Great Central
Corridor stock 1912

From about 1911 the Great Central introduced new corridor and non-corridor stock of a larger profile than that employed hitherto, 8ft 10½in wide over the bodies and usually 60ft long; door handles were recessed to give an overall width of 9ft. Features of the coaches were the vertical matchboarding below the waist, and the high elliptical roofs. They were among the heaviest of wooden-bodied British coaches and some types tared as much as 37tons. BELOW is a corridor composite. In 1915 J. G. Robinson, the GC's chief mechanical engineer, introduced an anti-collision device—corrugated steel interlocking fenders built into the coach ends (RIGHT). In a collision the fenders would engage and prevent telescoping; they were never put to a serious practical test and were later removed. [British Railways

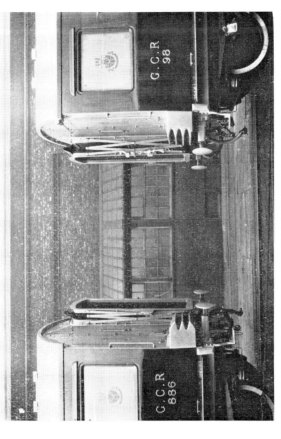

GN Railmotors
Sentinel cars

In 1905, in common with other railways, the GN introduced self-propelled steam railmotors; the engine units were separate from the coach, to which they were attached by an articulated coupling. The coach portion of the first GN railmotor had a low elliptical roof similar to that employed on GN stock for the previous 30 years, but the second, LEFT, introduced the high elliptical roof to GN carriage practice. In the mid 1920s the LNER again ventured into the steam railcar field, with Sentinel and Clayton chain or gear-driven steam cars. *Illustrated BELOW is Sentinel-Cammell 100 h.p. car TALLY-HO built in 1928 and which seated 59 passengers. By 1933 the LNER had 90 steam railcars in service.*

[British Railways

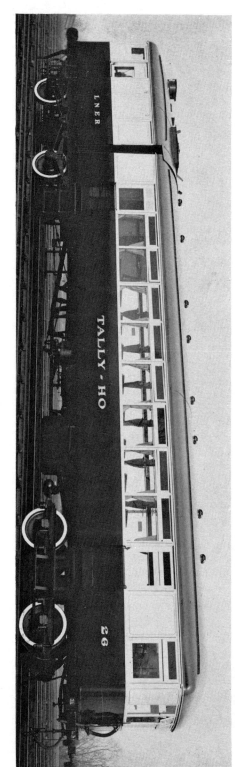

East Coast
Royal saloons 1908

In 1908/9 the Great Northern and North Eastern railways each built new 12-wheel saloons respectively for King Edward and Queen Alexandra as part of the new GN Royal train. Both coaches were 65ft 6in long over headstocks and 67ft over the bow ends of the body and were distinguished by their massive bowstring girder under-frames. Each had day and night accommodation; in both saloons the main bedroom could be converted into a dining room by an exchange of furniture. Special features included electric heating and lighting, including concealed tubular lights. RIGHT, is the interior of the King's saloon and, BELOW, the Queen's saloon; both are still in use for day journeys.

[British Railways; J. Scrace]

113

LNER Non-corridor stock 1924-39

The first Gresley LNER suburban designs were new four-coach articulated sets for GN services, almost identical to the GN-pattern quad-arts. Two coaches in each unit were 38ft 1¼in long, and the other two 43ft 6in. There were detail differences; the LNER sets were electrically instead of gas lit and doors had ventilators instead of top lights. Similar five coach quint-art sets, formed entirely of 43ft 6in coaches, were produced for Great Eastern line suburban services from Liverpool Street; they had Westinghouse brakes (only). Other LNER suburban stock was 51ft in length and included compartment and semi-corridor or lavatory types; some coaches were articulated in pairs. LEFT and BELOW are parts of a GE line quint-art, TOP RIGHT an eight coach train of Gresley twin-arts for the Cheshire Lines Committee, and, BELOW RIGHT, a 51ft semi-corridor lavatory composite.

LNER 1945-8
Non-corridors

Thompson non-corridor coaches built from 1945 until about 1951 were clearly based on Gresley designs in general layout but were 52ft 2½in long over headstocks and had steel panelled bodies with deeper quarterlights. None of the Thompson coaches was articulated. Earlier Thompson coaches had square cornered windows but later batches had the corners rounded to avoid corrosion. There were four basic types of Thompson coach, a third, brake composite, brake third (with varying numbers of compartments) and a semi-corridor lavatory composite; the last two are illustrated respectively BELOW and LEFT.

[D. L. Percival

ER
Southend stock 1954

For the first years of nationalisation, a steel shortage restricted BR's carriage building programme and coaches urgently needed to replace life-expired LTSR and Midland stock on the Fenchurch Street-Southend line could be obtained only by salvaging usable components from other withdrawn stock. Thus the steel underframes and bogies of Great Eastern 54ft suburban coaches, built just before Grouping and made redundant by the 1949 Shenfield electrification scheme, were reconditioned and given new timber-framed steel-panelled bodies of basically Thompson pattern, but designed for the longer underframes. Four types of coach were produced—brake third, third, open lavatory third and semi-open lavatory composite—close-coupled in units of four, with generally two units were coupled to run as an eight-coach train. The open lavatory third, with five-a-side seating, illustrated, was a type new to BR. [G. M. Kichenside; British Railways

LNER 1923-39 Corridor stock

Although Gresley produced new designs for the LNER from 1923, continuity in design could be traced back to the establishment of the general shape and contour of the first Gresley elliptical roof corridor coaches in 1906 and 30 or so years before that for the varnished teak finish and rectangular bodyside panelling and beading. Indeed Gresley continued to employ teak bodies until the second world war, although steel panelled coaches had appeared on the LNER in the mid 1930s, for timber bodied coaches could be produced more economically than steel at that time.
Gresley built numerous side-door coaches, but from

the end of the 1920s produced some end-door side-corridor vehicles and large numbers of end door open coaches. Most coaches were 60ft long over headstocks but some corridor coaches were produced on the shorter 51ft underframes. In the early 1930s the LNER conducted experiments in wireless reception on a Kings Cross-Leeds train; passengers could hire headphones from the dining car attendant. They were plugged into headphone points in the coach, connected to a wireless in the guards van which picked up a variety of programmes through a receiving aerial mounted along the carriage roof (TOP LEFT). LOWER LEFT is an open third built for the " East Anglian " service in 1929; right is a 51ft brake third and below a 60ft brake composite.

[British Railways; Eric Treacy; D. Percival

LNER
Tourist stock

In the mid-1930s Gresley produced several sets of excursion coaches known as the "Tourist stock", formed of twin articulated open third class coaches. Unusual were the plywood- (later, steel-) panelled bodies and the engine green and cream livery, which, although it had been adopted for the LNER's Sentinel and Clayton steam railcars, had not until then appeared on ordinary steam-hauled LNER coaching stock. In outline, too, they lacked the domed roofs of normal LNER corridor coaches and, indeed, set the general pattern for the high-speed streamlined train sets built in the following years. Trains were formed of 12-coach sets and included a 61ft 6in brake third at each end, two 61ft 6in buffet cars and four articulated twin-thirds, each 52ft long. Each coach was open throughout and had low-backed bucket seats, with tables to each bay. A single door gave access to each coach.

[British Railways

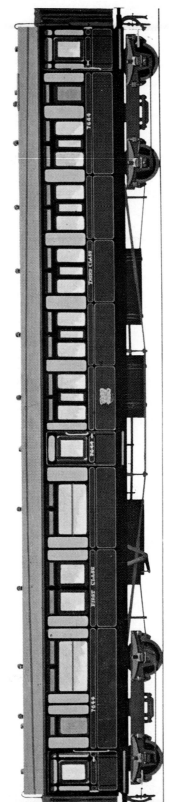

LNWR Oerlikon 57ft electric motor brake third built 1915

GWR 68ft "Dreadnought" corridor composite of 1905

SE&CR 44ft brake third built about 1901

123

1936

Railway carriage liveries (concluded)

unlikely railway colour scheme of brown and salmon pink, which varied in shade from coach to coach depending on the time since the coach was painted. The South Eastern & Chatham was a maroon line as far as its coaches were concerned, while the neighbouring Brighton line used varnished mahogany or umber brown.

Until the supersession of wooden bodies by steel panels in the late 1920s and early 1930s considerable work was entailed in painting carriages; some railways called for as many as 17 coats of primer, paint and varnish to achieve perfection in carriage livery. Indeed, some of the subtle livery tones could be obtained only by strict adherence to a specification which laid down exactly how many coats were to be applied and the preparation needed between each. Some liveries employed ornate lining on mouldings and around windows, doors and other bodyside protrusions, with, in some cases, two or even three contrasting edge linings.

The natural finish of varnished teak was a familiar sight in Eastern England for many years; indeed it was employed unbrokenly on the Great Northern and by its successor, the LNER, from about the 1870s until 1947. The LNER even used a grained finish on steel-panelled stock built just before and after the second world war. In contrast the LNER used distinctive liveries for its streamlined trains and for its Tyneside electric trains which were liveried in blue and white. Of the other three Group companies, the Great Western continued with chocolate and cream, the LMS inherited Midland crimson lake, which soon degenerated into a dull maroon, while the Southern adopted green, Olive green at first and the much brighter Malachite green from about 1938. Lining and embellishments were simplified; indeed the Southern later abandoned lining.

The formation of the unified British Railways has not yet seen a standard livery which has lasted for any length of time. The first standard crimson lake and cream lasted for about seven years, only to be replaced by maroon from about 1957 with revivals of Southern green, and chocolate and cream on the Western Region. Even the standard green used for diesel and electric multiple-units differs in shade from works to works. Now BR is to have a corporate image and more new liveries, in which blue and grey are to predominate. Surely the wheel has turned full circle. Illustrated in the centre pages are selected carriage liveries of pre-1922 companies to the present day.

124

LNER 1945-8
Corridor stock

Thompson's post-war corridor coaches showed marked differences from their Gresley predecessors. Gone were the varnished teak bodies and domed roofs of Gresley stock; in their place came neat steel-panelled designs with an unusual layout, for entry doors were placed between groups of compartments in such a way that to reach a compartment from a platform a passenger would have to pass no more than one other compartment. A distinguishing feature was the oval window of toilet compartments; most types were on 61ft 6in underframes, as for example the brake third, RIGHT, but the composites (BELOW) were on 58ft underframes.
[G. M. Kichenside

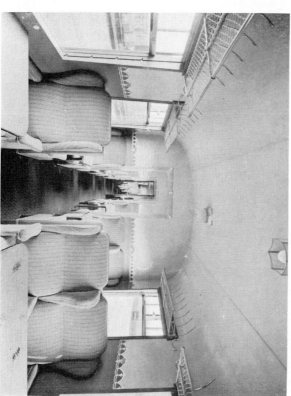

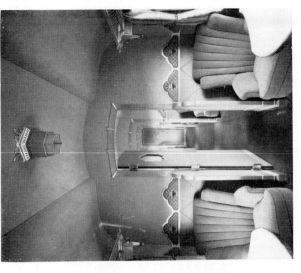

LNER
"Coronation" train 1937

In 1937 the LNER, following the success of its first streamlined train, "The Silver Jubilee" introduced in 1935, placed in service new sets for two more streamliners, the Kings Cross-Edinburgh "Coronation" and the Kings Cross-Leeds "West Riding". The trains for both services were articulated in twin sets and formed brake third and third, kitchen third and third, twin first, kitchen third and brake third, of the open pattern throughout; passengers had meals at their own seats. First class saloons with two-a-side seating had partitions dividing each bay into four-seat alcoves; the thirds had two-and-one seating and every bay was fitted with a table. The tables at double seats in the thirds had drop flaps at the edges to allow easier access to the window seats.

The coaches themselves were 56ft 2½in long and had timber-framed steel-panelled bodies. Particularly attention was paid to internal and external decor and the streamliners were quite unlike other LNER trains in external livery. The 1935 "Silver Jubilee" trains were in silver and grey, and the "Coronation" and "West Riding" trains in Marlborough grey for the upper panels and Garter blue below the waist. The body panelling in all the streamline trains was carried down to cover the solebars and underframe gear between the bogies, and rubber fairings filled the space between coaches. In summer the "Coronation" trains were

provided with an observation car 51ft 9in long, the observation ends of which was streamlined like the A4 Pacific locomotives used to haul the train.

TOP LEFT is the "Coronation" train including observation car, below it, to the left, is the interior of the observation car and, to the right, one of the third class saloons. RIGHT is one of the first class saloons. The streamlined trains were not revived after the second world war and the coaches were dispersed in ordinary trains. The twin open firsts ran for some years in the "Talisman" sets; the observation cars, rebuilt with new ends (BELOW), survive on the West Highland line in Scotland. [British Railways

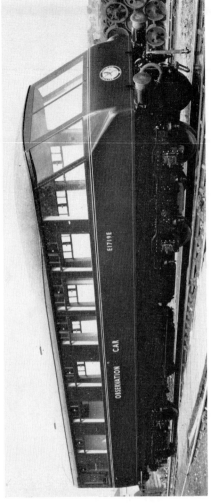

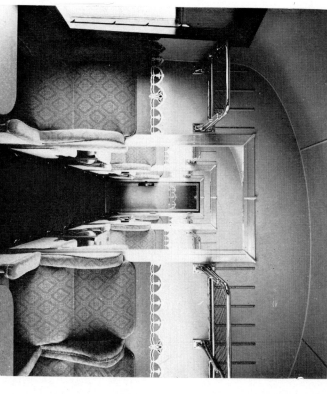

128

LNER
"Flying Scotsman"
"Hook Continental"
1938

The LNER streamlined trains were not the only ones to receive new sets of stock in 1938 and new trains were built for the "Flying Scotsman" (the third time since 1924), the "Hook Continental" and the "East Anglian train". The latter, like the streamliners, had open accommodation throughout and passengers dined at their own seats. But the "Hook Continental" and the "Flying Scotsman" trains included side corridor coaches and independent restaurant cars. Unlike the streamlined sets these trains were mostly formed of 61ft 6in stock, liveried in the normal varnished teak. Some coaches in the Flying Scotsman sets however, were 66ft 6in long. The "Hook" set included a third class brake but the remaining accommodation was of second and first class; both open first and open second class coaches had internal partitions dividing the bays into four- or six-seat alcoves.

The "Flying Scotsman" trains included triplet articulated dining sets, and buffet lounge cars. First class compartments seated four passengers and third class compartments six; pressure ventilation and double glazed windows were standard features. TOP LEFT is part of the "Hook Continental" set, and left below is the open second saloon in the "Hook" set. On this page are three views of the "Flying Scotsman".—RIGHT, the first class dining car, below right, the buffet lounge and, BELOW, a first class compartment.

[British Railways

LNER
Restaurant and buffet cars   1925-48

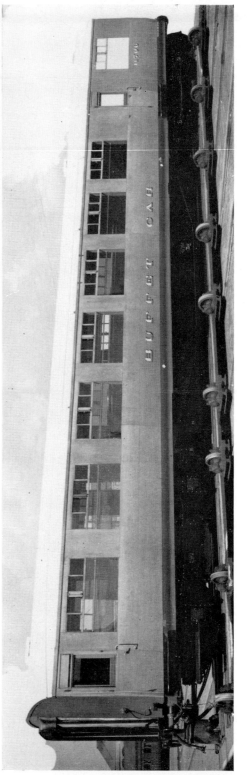

As we saw earlier, Gresley introduced his first all-electric kitchen car in a five-coach articulated dining car train built for the GN in 1921. Thereafter all-electric kitchens were standardised on the LNER for most catering vehicles. At first the kitchens were equipped for connection to a land-based electricity supply at terminal stations to avoid drawing on the car batteries while standing, but some cars had more powerful dynamos and batteries and did not need the landline connections. Gresley built several triplet articulated dining sets not only for the set named trains but ordinary expresses as well. They were formed of an open first and open third with a full kitchen in the centre (TOP LEFT). The two dining cars were 55ft 2½in long and the kitchen car 41ft but some of the triplet, dining sets were slightly longer with a 45ft kitchen car.

The LNER made extensive use of buffet cars which were capable of serving light snacks and main meals on the lighter cross-country trains, as for example the Newcastle-Carlisle service, and the Cambridge buffet expresses from Kings Cross. LEFT BELOW is a buffet-restaurant car built in the late 1930s; RIGHT and BELOW is the Thompson buffet lounge car built in 1948 for the new "Flying Scotsman" train composed entirely of Thompson stock.

[British Railways]

131

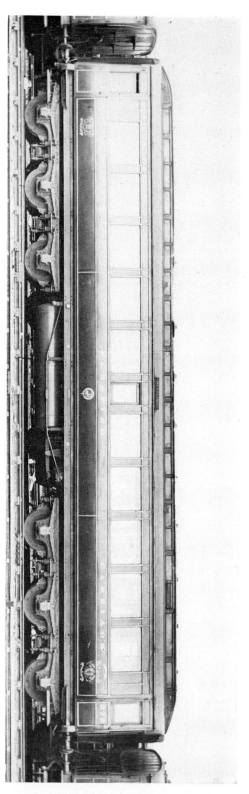

East Coast
Sleeping cars 1900-1948

By the end of the 1890s, following a variety of internal layouts in vogue in the preceding 20 years, what became the standard sleeping car layout of side corridor and transverse berths in compartments had become established. Bain on the North Eastern had introduced a non-gangwayed clerestory-roofed bogie sleeping car for the North Eastern in the mid-1890s, and by 1900 had developed a 55ft long 12-wheel gangwayed pattern containing two double berth compartments, five single berths, a half compartment for smokers, an attendant's compartment, and two toilets (TOP LEFT). Further improvements followed normal carriage development through the first years of the

present century. In 1922 Gresley introduced twin articulated first class sleepers for the East Coast Joint Stock (RIGHT) and individual cars at various times during the 1920s and 1930s. BELOW is a first class car of 1930. Similar four-berth cars with rug and pillow bedding were built for the introduction of third class sleeping facilities in 1928. LEFT BELOW is a Thompson 65ft third class sleeper of 1947, one of six, which, for a British railway, had the unique interior layout of four interlaced high and low level berths, providing single and double berth compartments, all with full bedding, luxury indeed for third class passengers.
[British Railways

NER and LNER
Electric stock 1904-37

In 1904 the North Eastern Railway inaugurated its Newcastle area electrification. Stock for the new services was 55ft long over headstocks and had straight matchboarded sides, clerestory roofs and end entrance vestibules with gates leading to open saloon accommodation. Coaches were of a variety of types, some all-third, some including first class, some with luggage compartments, and some with one or both ends with driving controls. In 1920 the NER placed in service new cars to replace 34 coaches lost in a carriage shed fire in 1918. The new stock resembled the old in many ways, but had elliptical roofs and was painted in NER maroon livery instead of the red and cream adopted for the original stock.

In 1937 the 1904 stock had become life expired and Gresley ordered

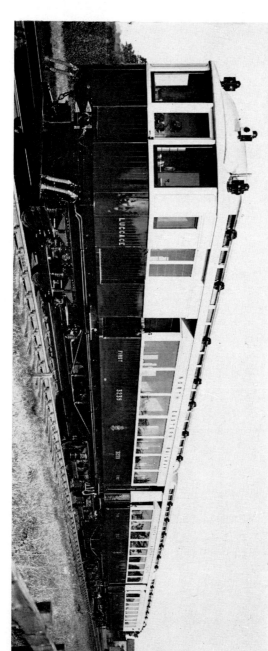

new electric coaches for North Tyneside services consisting of twin articulated coaches, each of 55ft 9in in length. They had steel sides and internally were fitted with bucket seats. Entrance to the coaches was by end vestibules fitted with hand-worked sliding doors. From the Grouping in 1923 until 1937 the LNER had used artificial varnished teak livery for the Tyneside electric stock but revived red and cream for the new 1937 stock and for the 1920 stock which was refurbished for use on the newly-electrified South Tyneside lines. Four years later the livery was altered to blue and off-white. On the facing page is an NER 1904 three-car set and ABOVE the interior of a third class saloon. RIGHT is a 1920 stock train as refurbished in 1937 and BELOW an eight-car train of LNER 1937 articulated stock.

[British Railways

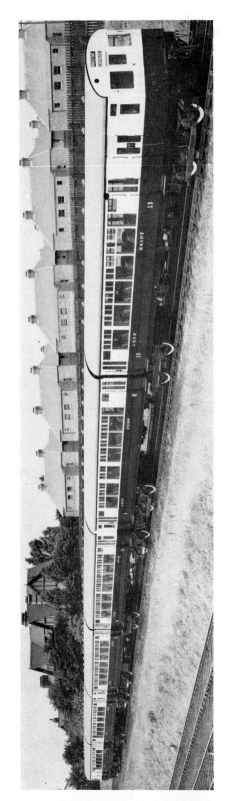

GWR stock
1860-1900

Among coaches taken over by the Great Western were those of its allied West Country companies; the Cornwall Railway broad gauge first (BELOW) of the 1850s was inherited by the Great Western in 1889 and survived until the abandonment of the broad gauge in 1892. LEFT is illustrated a variety of non-bogie coaches built in the 1870s and 1890s for the GWR; nearest the camera is a main line six-wheel tri-composite of the 1870s and including a luggage compartment; next to it is a four-wheel 28ft London area suburban composite built in the early 1890s with its characteristic round top doors, for through working over the Metropolitan line to the City; beyond is an 1880s four-wheel first for branch duties. This rake is seen here in about 1910 in the all-brown livery of the period at Newton Abbot.

[Locomotive Publishing Company

GWR 1880 Four-wheel stock

Until the last years of the 19th century the GWR continued building four-wheelers for branch service, as for example the brake third, and first and second class composite, illustrated RIGHT and BELOW. In design and profile they were not unlike the bogie clerestory stock of the 1880s with similar body panelling, turnunder ends and three-radius arc roof corresponding in profile to the lower deck roof of GW clerestory vehicles. Notice the solebar branding allocating the coaches to specific services. [British Railways

GWR.
Absorbed stock

The Great Western was least affected by the Grouping in 1923 and carriage design was subject to a continuation of policy. Nevertheless the Great Western inherited a considerable amount of stock from the companies it absorbed at or before the Grouping. Much of it was antiquated and was soon broken up. Later pre-Grouping coaches of the minor GW constituents lasted well into the 1930s and a few even into BR days.

138

TOP LEFT is a Rhymney Railway 47ft 9in-long third, dating from the first world war period; it was open internally and divided into two saloons with entry through doors at the ends of the saloon. It retained wooden seats until its withdrawal. It was photographed here in 1954 as a workmen's coach on the Caerphilly Works train. BELOW LEFT is a Cambrian Railways corridor third, seen in GW livery in 1935. TOP RIGHT is a Barry Railway brake third built by the Birmingham Railway Carriage & Wagon Co. in 1920 and condemned in 1959. BELOW is part of the Swindon dump of condemned stock soon after 1923 with, from left to right, a former Midland brake composite from the Midland & South Western Junction, a Cambrian Railways six-wheel third, a Lambourn Valley four-wheel end balcony open third and a Cambrian lavatory composite.

[T. J. Edgington; H. F. Wheeller; R. O. Tuck; British Railways

GWR Clerestory stock 1888-1905

William Dean GW locomotive superintendent also responsible for carriage design, re-introduced the clerestory roof to GW coaches in the early 1870s (its original appearance had been on some broad gauge saloons of 1838). The clerestory roof continued in use on many GW coaches until about 1904 when Churchward, who succeeded Dean, abandoned it in favour of the high elliptical roof on his new Dreadnought stock (see page 143).

In 1892 the GW placed in service on the Paddington-Birkenhead run the first British side-corridor train with through gangways, although since the intervening gangway doors were kept locked passengers could not pass from coach to coach. The flexible gangways between the coaches were at one side. Illustrated BELOW is an early GW corridor second, part of a set train built after the pioneer set in 1893. A feature of Dean's clerestory corridor coaches of all one class, that is all-third, all-second, and all-first, was the inclusion of a two- or three-bay open saloon at one end of the coach for smokers, since smoking was forbidden in the side corridor compartments. At the top of this page is

a third class saloon in which it will be noticed that the seat ends had no arm rests.

It was soon clear that side-gangways brought operating problems if coaches were turned, and the flexible gangway was placed centrally on subsequent stock, with the exception of post office coaches, many of which still have side gangways. On this page are two of Dean's later

[Concluded on page 142]

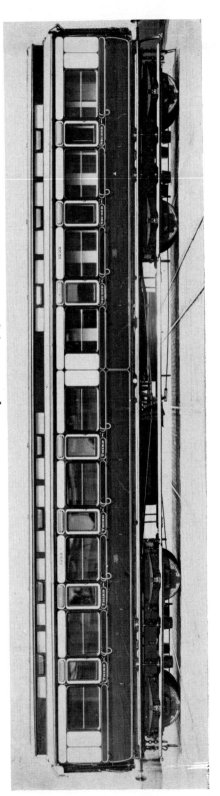

GWR clerestory stock 1888-1905

concluded

corridor vehicles, at the top a first/second class composite and below it a second/third class composite. At the top of this page is a 58ft non-gangwayed semi-corridor brake tricomposite of 1895, with four third class compartments linked to two toilets, one second and 1½ firsts with individual toilets. Below is a vehicle unusual in British practice—a travelling post office coach, including mail pick-up and set-down apparatus, with passenger accommodation. It was a convertable brake third built in 1888 for broad gauge services; it had a side gangway at the sorting end only.

[British Railways

GWR 1905
Dreadnought stock

Churchward abandoned the clerestory roof soon after he took office and introduced the high elliptical roof in some stock which was the largest ever to run in Britain, the "Dreadnought" stock of 1905 so called after the warships of that name with which they were contemporary. The various types of Dreadnought coach differed slightly in length from the 68ft of the composites to 70ft of the brake thirds. Features of the Dreadnoughts were large end and centre doors, a corridor which changed sides half way, and poky little third class compartments only 5ft 6in between partitions. BELOW is a Dreadnought third and ABOVE a 12-wheel first class sleeper built in 1907. [British Railways

GWR 1908-20 Toplight stock

The Dreadnought vehicles just described introduced top lights—small additional windows above the main windows—to GW carriage practice and appeared as a standard feature on GW coaches from then until about 1919. The "toplight" stock, as it was known, covered a variety of types, both corridor and non-corridor, and of different lengths. The brake tri-composite (LEFT), a "70 footer", had a panelled wooden body with recessed doors, but later coaches had steel sided bodies with lining to represent panels. BELOW is a 57ft corridor third, a type built more-or-less throughout the period; TOP RIGHT is one of the low roof 48ft "City" set thirds of 1919 for London suburban services, and, below, a 70ft brake third for Birmingham suburban services.

[British Railways

GWR 1924-9 Corridor stock

Collett succeeded Churchward as GW chief mechanical engineer in 1922 and continued building coaches of the same general pattern as the last Churchward coaches but with important differences; toplights were abandoned, steel, almost flush, sides were standardised and chocolate and cream livery was reintroduced. Windows were not quite flush with the sides and were recessed by about an inch. Collett turned out some 70ft stock (LEFT is a corridor third) between 1922 and 1924 mostly for London-South Wales services, but thereafter standardised 57 and 60ft coaches. BELOW

is a 57ft composite of 1923. Collett experimented with articulated coaches in some set trains built from 1925; they were eight-coach formations comprising twin brake first and first, triplet first diner, kitchen and third diner, and triplet two thirds and brake third. Illustrated ABOVE is the third class triplet (note the tail and side lamps) and BELOW is the triplet diner. All the coaches were rebuilt on individual bogies a few years later.

[D. Rouse, British Railways

GWR 1924-33
Two-coach "B sets"

In the 1920s the Great Western put into traffic a large number of permanently coupled two-coach non-corridor trains known as B sets. They were largely employed in the Bristol Division but also on main line stopping and branch services in other areas. There were several batches of B sets differing in detail; the earliest were 57ft vehicles, the later ones 60ft; some had flat ends others bow ends. Each set was formed of two identical brake composites containing one first and six third class compartments, although later batches had one compart-

ment fewer. In the earliest sets the first class compartments were at the adjacent coach ends but the later sets had the first class compartment in the coach centre. The B sets were often used on main line stopping services for which corridor stock would have been preferable; the Great Western did not build any non-corridor lavatory stock after Dean's clerestory vehicles of this type. ABOVE is a B set with first class compartments at the coach ends; in the set BELOW the first class compartment is at the centre of each coach. [British Railways

148

GWR
Corridor stock 1929-34

From 1929 GW carriage design was taken a stage further when flush-sided steel-panelled bodies appeared, although basic coach layouts changed little and were still based on Churchward's toplight stock. Three types of stock appeared at this time differing in dimensions; two were on 59ft 10in underframes and were respectively 9ft 5in and 9ft 3in wide over body—the former built specifically for the "Cornish Riviera" service—and the latter for general service. The third type was on the 56ft 10½in underframe with 9ft wide body.

The two wide-body types had recessed door and grab handles; the grab handles of the 9ft stock were of a similar short vertical pattern instead of the "C" shaped handles employed for many years until then. Later batches of this type were also notable for the alteration in corridor side design, which now provided only four external doors instead of doors opposite every compartment. ABOVE is a 9ft 5in wide coach of 1929 and BELOW a 9ft 3in wide third of 1933. Notice the simplified livery compared with the mid-1920s coaches opposite. [British Railways

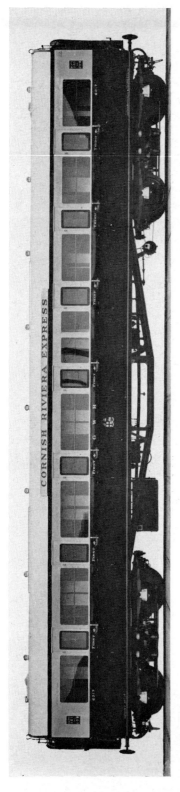

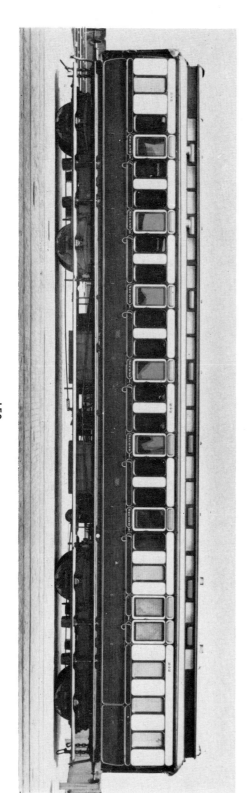

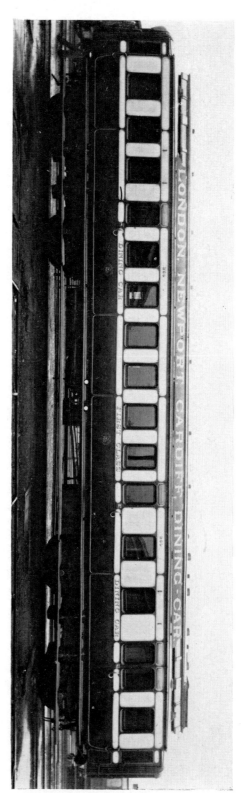

GWR 1896-1905
Restaurant cars

The Great Western was not one of the first companies to provide dining facilities on its trains; indeed while trains were required to make the compulsory stop at Swindon for refreshment purposes it had no need to. But even after the refreshment stop had been abolished in 1895 it was in no hurry to introduce dining cars extensively. TOP LEFT is one of the earliest cars, first class only, and converted from centre to side gangway for the South Wales service in 1896. BELOW LEFT is the first GW buffet car built at the turn of the century. It was more exactly a pantry car, for it did not have a buffet counter as is known today. The remainder of the coach consisted of open second class accommodation. RIGHT and BELOW are the interior and exterior of a Churchward Dreadnought diner built in about 1907. Later the Great Western standardised composite dining cars with a central kitchen and first and third class dining saloons at each end.

[British Railways

GWR
Buffet car 1934

In an attempt to provide a more flexible catering service and in particular the service of hot snacks, with the minimum of staff, the Great Western introduced new buffet cars in the mid-1930s. The main feature internally was the long buffet counter running for almost the whole length of the car. Bar stools were provided along part of the counter to allow passengers to have meals in the car but there were no other seats or tables. Passengers requiring only drinks and sandwiches could buy them at the counter and take them to their own seats. The buffet cars were employed on ordinary services running over the shorter distances, for example London and Bristol, at times when full meals were not required. A similar vehicle to the one illustrated LEFT and BELOW has been preserved at the Museum of British Transport at Clapham

[British Railways]

GWR
Open stock 1935

In the mid-1930s the Great Western, like the LNER, built some sets of open stock specially for excursion work to counter the effects of road competition. Normally, except for dining vehicles and the later Dean clerestory coaches, the GWR did not use open vehicles, and the excursion sets were usually confined to that sort of work; occasionally however they were used on summer Saturday reliefs. Several batches, differing in detail, were built from 1935. The first, 60ft long, had two toilets at one end with external doors at the opposite end of the coach and in the centre (RIGHT and BELOW). Later coaches, 1ft longer had a most unusual arrangement of toilets placed in diagonally opposite corners of the coach balanced by external doors at the remaining corners, with another set of doors in the centre of the coach. This layout has recently been revived by BR in its XP64 train.

153

GWR
"Super saloons" 1931
Centenary stock 1935

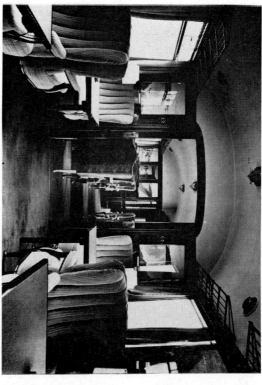

We have already noted the Dreadnought coaches of 1905, the largest ever to run in Britain, but they were not the widest. That honour now goes to some London Transport underground stock, but for many years the Great Western "Super saloons" of 1931 and the "Centenary" stock of 1935 were the widest, with a body width of 9ft 7in, and recessed end doors. Naturally they were restricted in their spheres of operation, and were not permitted north of Wolverhampton or Hereford, over the Eastern and Western Valleys lines from Newport or over certain other sections in South Wales.

The "Super saloons" were designed for the Plymouth-London boat trains; their appointments were not unlike Pullman cars and they commanded a supplementary fare. Seating was in loose armchairs arranged as one-and-one or two-and-one on each side of the centre passageway. All were named after members of the Royal family. Two cars, of which Princess Elizabeth (LEFT LOWER) was one, were rebuilt in 1935 as restaurant cars with a kitchen and pantry and 24 seats. TOP LEFT, is the interior of Prince of Wales.

In 1935 came the "Centenary" stock for the "Cornish Riviera", 60ft long with six types of coach built to the same general profile: brake third, third, composite, brake composite, kitchen first and third diner. These coaches, like the super saloons and the open excursion stock had large drop windows in each compartment or bay, but were later rebuilt with fixed windows and sliding window ventilators in the top of the frame. ABOVE is a Centenary stock third as altered and BELOW a brake composite as built. [British Railways

GWR Slip coaches

The Great Western was one of the most prolific users of slip coaches—coaches detached at speed from the rear of non-stopping expresses to serve intermediate stations. The slip coach was detached by a guard who travelled in the coach; he operated a lever which opened the

hinged coupling drawhook and parted the vacuum brake pipes which were resealed by special valves. Great Western slips operated singly or in trains of up to three or four vehicles with a slip brake leading. Most GW slips were double ended and non-gangwayed, but some had gangways at the non-slip end with a slip brake compartment at the other end only. ABOVE is a non-corridor slip brake composite originally built in the 1880s as a tri-composite. BELOW is a slip brake composite of the mid-1930s.

[British Railways

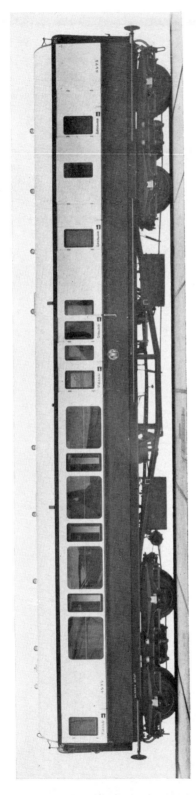

GWR Corridor stock 1936-48

The design of GW corridor stock took a further step forward in the mid-1930s when side doors to each compartment were abandoned for end doors and access to compartments by the corridor. The first

vehicles of this type, built in 1936, retained a droplight between the large corridor windows, but later batches had only large corridor windows matching those of the compartments. Indeed coaches built between 1936 and 1938 showed a number of variations in design details, not least being the different lengths (which varied from 57ft 2in to 60ft 11in over body) depending on the coach type. A body width of 9ft was standardised. ABOVE is a 60ft 11in brake third of 1936. GW post war stock built from 1947 until 1951, of unified length with a 63ft underframe, was distinguished by a roof domed at the ends rather like that of Gresley's LNER stock. Destination boards were placed above the windows on the bodyside instead of on the roof. BELOW is a Hawksworth corridor third of 1948.

[British Railways

GWR Non-corridor stock 1937-53

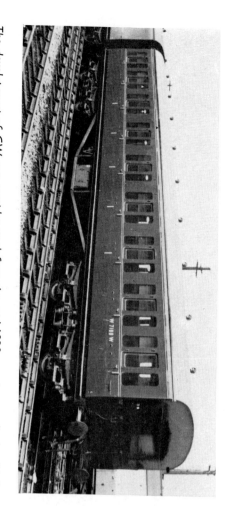

The development of GW non-corridor stock from the mid-1930s, as in earlier periods, followed the design trends of corridor stock. Steel-panelled flush-sided bodies were standardised, and the quarterlights and door droplights gradually became deeper; like the corridor stock built between 1935 and 1940, lengths of pre-war vehicles varied according to type—55ft 3in for thirds, 57ft for brake thirds and brake composites and 59ft 3in for composites. All had bodies 9ft wide at the waist or an inch less in some cases. Unique, however, were six

brake thirds and one third (illustrated BELOW) built in 1939 for the Burry Port and Gwendraeth Valley line in South Wales which had severely restricted headroom. These coaches, otherwise of normal design, but 8ft 8in wide, had low arc roofs, reminiscent of the type common in the late 1800s. Post-war GW suburban stock was mostly standardised on 63ft underframes; the bodysides were almost flat, with little turnunder below the waist. ABOVE is a post-war 63ft composite built in 1953.
[British Railways: P. J. Sharpe

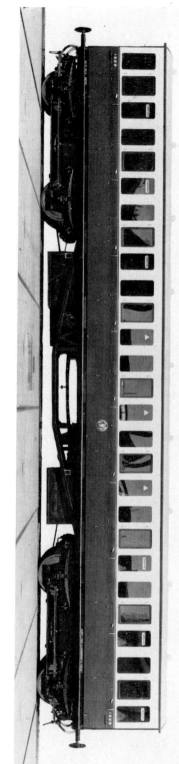

GWR
Railmotors

The Great Western was one of the pioneers in the introduction of rail motor units in an attempt to reduce operating costs on lightly used local and branch services. In 1903 the GW placed in service its first railmotor on the Gloucester-Chalford stopping service, and in the next few years introduced them all over the system. As we have

already seen, railmotors took one of two forms, the railway carriage attached to a separate locomotive unit, and the fully enclosed power unit operating within the coach body. Great Western railmotors were of the latter type. They varied in design and length but nearly all were of the open saloon pattern with end or central doors. Most of the railmotors were massive 70 footers. Similar driving trailer coaches built to run with the railmotors were designed so that the concluded on page 160

GWR Railmotors concluded

motor unit could be controlled from the trailer when the latter was being propelled. But the lack of power of the small steam engine unit, although more economical than a normal locomotive was not really adequate for the haulage of trailers.

At the top of page 159 is a typical GW railmotor and trailer, and below on the same page is an experimental trailer car with side sliding doors to each set of seats. Some of the railmotors and trailers were rebuilt as ordinary push-pull trailers, typical of which is the push-pull train illustrated BELOW. LEFT is the interior of a later GW push-pull trailer. For some services the Great Western introduced push-pull trains adapted from ordinary compartment stock ABOVE RIGHT. BELOW RIGHT is a railmotor of the Taff Vale. [British Railways; L.P.C.

160

GWR
Petrol and diesel
railcars

The Great Western was also one of the pioneers in the introduction of the internal combustion engine for rail use. In 1912 it placed in service a four-wheel 40-seat petrol-electric car on the Windsor branch, a vehicle quite unlike a GW coach in appearance (LEFT); it was powered by a Maudslay 40 h.p. petrol engine. The experiment was clearly not successful, for little more was done at that time, but, 20 years later, it was a different story when the Great Western, in conjunction with AEC, introduced the first of its 38 diesel-

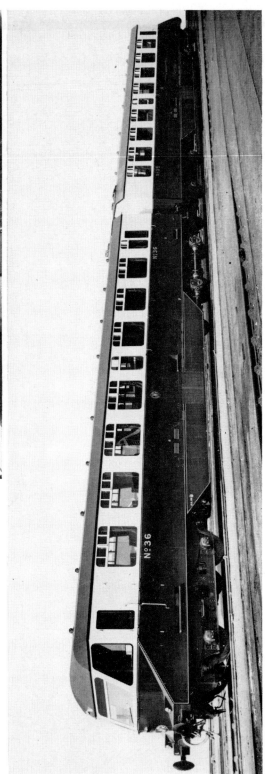

engined railcars. The first batch of cars were stream-lined, 62ft long, and seated variously from 40 to 70 passengers. A few included toilet and buffet facilities. The first were placed in service between Birmingham and Cardiff on express duty, for which they commanded a supplement of 2s 6d. LEFT BELOW is one of these cars at Cardiff.

The later batch of cars was more angular in appearance and four ran as two twin sets gangwayed together; they included buffet and toilet facilities (RIGHT and BELOW). Most of the GW cars were later employed on branch and main line stopping services. [British Railways

GWR Narrow gauge coaches

At the Grouping the Great Western inherited several Welsh narrow gauge lines, among them the 1ft 11½in gauge Vale of Rheidol line at Aberystwyth and the 2ft 6in gauge Welshpool & Llanfair line of the Cambrian Railways. The latter lost its passenger service in 1931 but the line is now run by a new preservation operating company and passenger services have been restored. BELOW is an original W&L brake composite. LEFT is an enclosed third class coach of the Vale of Rheidol at the time of grouping. This line is now BR's only narrow gauge line and is included in the London Midland Region.

[British Railways

GWR Dyna-mometer car Royal saloon

Last in the selection of Great Western coaches are the dynamometer car, RIGHT, built by Churchward in 1903 and Queen Victoria's saloon seen BELOW in the condition in which it was built in 1873 with a fixed eight-wheel arrangement. The coach, 43ft long, was equipped soon after with Dean's short wheelbase bogies. A feature was the bulge of the central saloon where the body was wider and higher than at the ends. The coach was rebuilt with longer end vestibules and ante-rooms in 1897 and was broken up in 1912. The dynamometer car lasted until 1965 but has since been privately preserved.

[D. L. Percival; L.P.C.

LSWR 1895-1915
Non-corridors

During the 1890s and the first few years of the present century the London & South Western built a large quantity of non-corridor lavatory stock for long distance express services, and later for main line stopping trains. Typical were the four-coach (later three-coach) sets for general use throughout the system; illustrated, LEFT, is a composite and, BELOW, a brake third from one of these sets, dating from the early years of the present century. Both had 56ft by 8ft wide bodies.
[G. M. Kichenside

LSWR 1905-22
Corridor stock

The LSW was one of the last companies to introduce gangwayed corridor stock on long distance services. After a tentative essay with through gangways in a dining car train formed of older converted saloon stock in 1901, corridor stock made a more general appearance on the LSW from about 1905; LSW corridor coaches were similar to contemporary non-corridor stock, with flattened elliptical roofs and neat panelled bodies usually 56ft long and 8ft 6in wide, 6in wider than the non-corridor vehicles. ABOVE is a train of this stock. RIGHT is a brake first representing the last style of LSW coach design, a steel panelled vehicle 57ft long by 9ft wide with double framed bogies and guard's doors angled inwards towards the coach ends. These coaches, built in the early 1920s, were known as "ironclads".

[British Railways; D. Cullum

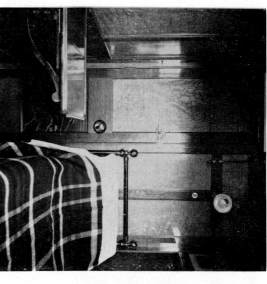

LSWR
Sleeping
and dining
cars
1901-8

Dining facilities on LSW trains other than those provided by Pullman cars made their appearance in some kitchen brake vans employed with rebuilt saloon coaches in 1901. The general introduction of LSW restaurant cars dates from about 1905; the cars themselves were generally similar to ordinary LSW stock but were graced with a clerestory roof which stood out above the flattened roofs of ordinary coaches. BELOW is the exterior of an LSW diner and on the facing page, right, is the first class saloon. Later, some went to the War Department and ended their careers on the Longmoor Military Railway (RIGHT).

In 1908 the LSW introduced four first class sleepers (facing page lower) to overnight Plymouth-London services. They contained seven single and two double berths. Unusual were the removable brass-framed bedsteads. (Facing page, left.) Three years later, they were sold to the Great Western who rebuilt one of the double compartments into a single and added an attendant's compartment. Two were later destroyed in a fire at Swindon. [British Railways; G. M. Kichenside

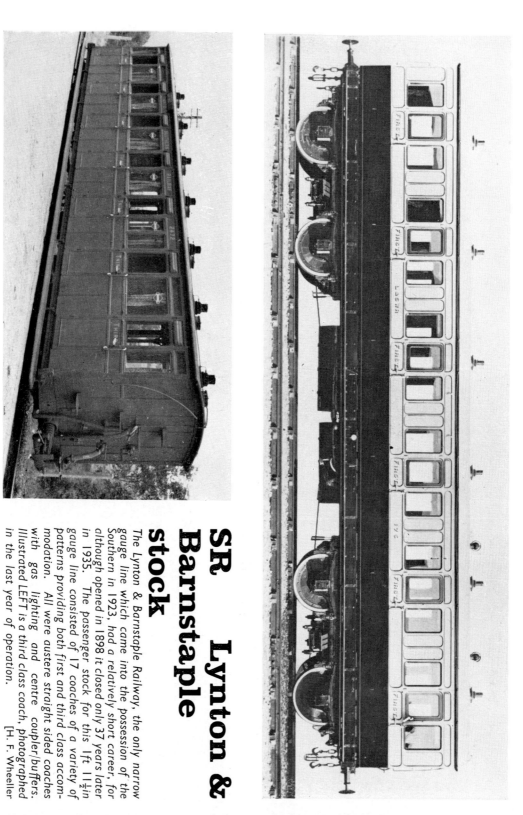

SR Lynton & Barnstaple stock

The Lynton & Barnstaple Railway, the only narrow gauge line which came into the possession of the Southern in 1923, had a relatively short career, for although opened in 1898 it closed only 37 years later in 1935. The passenger stock for this 1ft 11½in gauge line consisted of 17 coaches of a variety of patterns providing both first and third class accommodation. All were austere straight sided coaches with gas lighting and centre coupler/buffers. Illustrated LEFT is a third class coach, photographed in the last year of operation.

[H. F. Wheeller

LSWR
Early
bogie stock

The LSW was well to the fore in the introduction of bogie stock, which appeared in the 1880s. The first bogie coaches were comparatively short, no more than 45ft long, 8ft wide, with a low arc roof and gas lighting. Illustrated LEFT is a full first of the late 1880s.

[Locomotive Publishing Company]

LSWR
railmotors

The LSW, like many other companies between 1900 and 1910 took up the railmotor idea for the operation of branch and main line stopping services. LSW railmotors were of several patterns; the earliest, built for joint service with the LBSC on the Fratton-Southsea branch, employed a separate although enclosed locomotive unit. In later units the locomotive bogie was mounted within the coach body as in the railcar ABOVE. All had been withdrawn by the end of the first world war and the coach portions converted into push-pull trailers (LEFT).

[R. C. Riley]

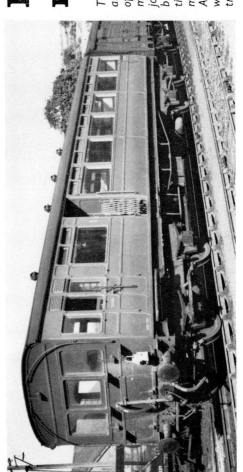

SER stock 1890-1900

The South Eastern Railway was also an early user of bogie coaches, the first of which it placed in service in the late 1870s. However, four- and six-wheel coaches continued to be built for main line and suburban services until the turn of the century. Typical of SER stock of the late 1800s is the six-wheel third of about 1890 seen LEFT as a lavatory third, with one of the compartments rebuilt as two toilets. BELOW is a 44ft bogie first/second composite of 1900 built soon after the working agreement with the London, Chatham & Dover came into force.

[British Railways: G. M. Kichenside

172

SE&C stock 1899-1905

The South Eastern & Chatham did not make extensive use of corridor stock; indeed its only corridor coaches were the 15 corridor brake tri-composites of three different patterns (BELOW) built in about 1907 for through workings between the Kent Coast and the Midlands, and the stock built in 1921/2 for Continental services. Otherwise the SE&C employed non-corridor stock, some with between-compartment toilets or short internal corridors. An example of SEC non-corridor stock of this period is the two-compartment lavatory brake second (RIGHT) built as part of a boat train set in 1905.

[G. M. Kichenside]

SE&C stock 1915-20

For general use the SEC built large numbers of three-coach Trio sets between 1905 and 1918, the brake coaches being distinguished with birdcage roof lookouts. Earliest sets had 50ft and 54ft coaches but the final type had 60ft coaches. Of the latter the final version had the birdcage suppressed (ABOVE). Three-class accommodation was provided and some compartments had access to toilets. BELOW is one of a large number of 60ft thirds built by the SE&C in its last years; they were planned for conversion as electric stock but, in the event, they remained steam hauled throughout their careers. [G. M. Kichenside

SE&C
Railmotors

The South Eastern & Chatham also employed rail-motors in the early years of the present century with eight units for the Sheppey Light Railway and other branches. But like those of other companies the railmotors were not an outstanding success and they were later rebuilt as push-pull coaches running in pairs. Four coaches were articulated as two twin sets. In each pair one of the guard's and drivers' compart-ments remained in use as such, but the other was fitted with seats for passengers. ABOVE is one of the units as built and, RIGHT, two former railmotor coaches in their last years. [British Railways; G. M. Kichenside]

SER Hastings and Folkestone cars 1892-7

In the 1890s the South Eastern Railway, produced two luxury trains which contrasted with the normally austere SER ordinary stock. In 1892 new first class drawing room cars 51ft 3in long by 8ft 4¾in wide built by the Gilbert Car Company in America were introduced.   Internally they had arm chairs in large open saloons.   The cars at first ran singly but in 1896 were formed into a single eight coach train, rebuilt with three-class accommodation and placed on the Hastings service.   In 1897 the SER placed in service on the Folkestone run some more parlour cars, this time built by the Metropolitan Carriage & Wagon Co, with one exception.   They were 56ft 1in long and 8ft 5in wide. Both types of car were later taken over by the Pullman Car Co.   Illustrated LEFT is a drawing room car of 1892 and BELOW part of the 1897 train, including a brake third with part clerestory birdcage roof.

[Locomotive Publishing Co.

SE&C 1921 Continental stock

In the last year of its existence the South Eastern & Chatham built its only corridor stock other than the brake tri-composites of 1907. The 1921/2 corridor stock was quite unlike anything else ever built for the SE&C and acquired the nickname of the "Continental" stock, partly because it was employed on Continental services and partly because the coaches looked rather Continental in appearance. They had flat

sides, matchboarded below the waist, were 8ft wide over the body and mounted on 62ft underframes. The high elliptical roof prevented the use of a birdcage lookout, so beloved by the SE&C, but the brake firsts had a small saloon, another feature commonly found on SEC first class compartment coaches. First class compartments seated four, and second and third class compartments six. The brake coaches were unusual in being gangwayed only at the non-brake end. ABOVE is a corridor third and LEFT a corridor brake first. Unusual, too, for the period was the lack of side doors with entry to the coach through end doors.

[D. Cullum; G. M. Kichenside

177

LBSC Four-wheel stock 1890

The LBSCR was another of the London lines carrying heavy suburban traffic in four-wheel stock marshalled in close-coupled sets, until the turn of the century. Most LBSCR stock at this time was only 8ft wide, because of tight clearances but just after 1900 R. J. Billinton introduced a train of wide-body four-wheelers; it was so restricted in route availability that it was not perpetuated. Illustrated on this page are LBSC four-wheel suburban coaches of the 1880s and 1890s, LEFT a set which survived in the Isle of Wight until the early 1930s and, BELOW, a close view of an LBSC third seen here in the Lancing Works train.

[O. J. Morris, courtesy J. L. Smith; L.P.C.

LBSC "Balloon" stock 1905

In contrast in 1905 the LBSCR turned out the first of its high roof "Balloon" stock, so called because of the roof profile.   This stock, the largest in normal service on the LBSCR and used mainly for express services, had 8ft 6in wide bodies and the length varied from 54ft to 56ft according to type.   The high roof profile, how-ever, brought restrictions in its use and, as a result, the Balloon stock was not perpetuated; the LBSC returned to the normal low arc roof until the end of its existence. The Balloon roof was also applied to some LBSC push-pull coaches.   RIGHT is a push-pull coach coupled to an ordinary low roof vehicle and, BELOW, is a Newhaven boat train formed of Balloon stock.

[British Railways; L.P.C.

LBSC Bogie stock 1901-22

A feature of LBSC stock until the end of the separate existence of the company, was the use of the low arc roof, abandoned by most companies soon after the turn of the century, although as we have just seen, the LBSC tried a high elliptical roof in the middle of the first decade.   Bogie suburban block trains appeared in 1901 (BELOW), generally seven coach formations with accommodation for all three classes.   The brake coaches sported large end windows in the guard's van, as in the earlier four-wheelers.   LEFT is a main line lavatory composite dating from about 1910.

[L.P.C.; O. J. Morris

180

SR Isle of Wight stock

The railways of the Isle of Wight have always been repositories for old coaches; for many years the Island carriage stock included old four-wheel LBSC coaches long after such things had disappeared from the mainland. Today the surviving coaches on the Island are of two patterns, former SE&C vehicles distinguished by their flattened elliptical roofs, and former LBSC bogie stock with their low arc roofs. Most Island stock has undergone rebuilding; the composite BELOW is a former SEC 54ft lavatory composite which has been rebuilt with a large third class saloon compartment in place of two firsts and two toilets. RIGHT is a former LBSC 54ft brake third on the Island. [G. M. Kichenside]

LBSC Electric stock 1908-28

The stock for the LBSC's electrified South London line, the first of the LBSC suburban lines to be converted to the a.c. overhead system, consisted of three coach sets of wide body stock, 60ft in length (BELOW). Later LBSC a.c. sets had 8ft wide bodies; with the abandonment of the a.c. system, the LBSC a.c. stock was rebuilt for d.c. use; many LBSC steam stock coaches also were adapted for electric working and survived in this form until the late 1950s. LEFT, is a motor brake composite of an LBSC-bodied d.c. electric suburban set. Some of these coaches were formed by mounting old four- and six-wheel bodies in pairs or in pieces on new underframes. [R. C. Riley collection; G. M. Kichenside

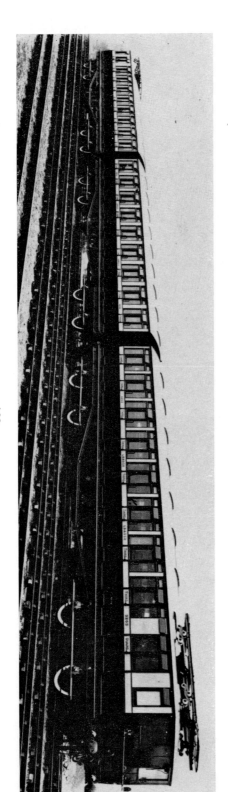

LSWR Waterloo
& City stock 1898

In 1898 the Waterloo & City line was opened between Waterloo and the Bank, and a few years later was taken over by the LSWR. The original cars to work the Waterloo & City were built in America and assembled at Eastleigh. The photograph, RIGHT, shows the rather austere interior of one of the cars, with its plywood seat backs. BELOW is a general view of a Waterloo & City train showing the original formation of motor car, two trailers and another motor car. Later, some motor coaches were adapted to run singly in off-peak hours. The cars had end gates supplemented by hand worked sliding doors on the motor coaches.

[British Railways

LSWR bogie blocks 1903 electrics 1915

In 1903 the LSW introduced its four-coach bogie block sets, which, during the first years of the present century, quickly replaced all the old four- and six-wheelers in London suburban services. For electrification in 1915 the bogie block sets were rebuilt into three-coach electric units. The driving cabs were given a distinguishing V-shaped front end. Although at first retaining the same 49 and 51ft length of the original bogie block coaches, the SR lengthened the coaches on new 62ft underframes in later years. BELOW is an original steam-hauled bogie block set of 1903 and, LEFT, the front end of a 1915 rebuilt electric multiple-unit.

[G. M. Kichenside; J. L. Smith

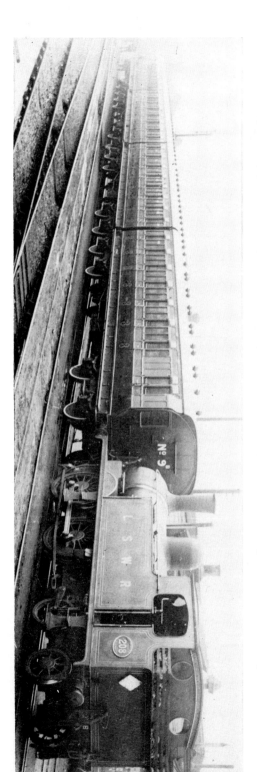

184

SR 1928-37
Rebuilt stock

With the exception of two batches of stock built for the Guildford and Orpington electrification schemes in 1925, all SR suburban electric stock built until 1941 was obtained by rebuilding pre-grouping steam coaches into electric vehicles. This was often no mere adaptation by the fitting of control cables and air brakes; in most cases it involved the combination of two or more carriage bodies or parts of bodies, some previously four- or six-wheelers, on new 62ft bogie underframes. Stock from all three principal Southern constituents was thus converted and there were many detail differences. RIGHT is the motor brake third of a two coach 2-NOL set of 1937 rebuilt from LSW steam stock and, BELOW, a three-coach set of former SEC stock converted in 1928. [G. M. Kichenside; British Railways

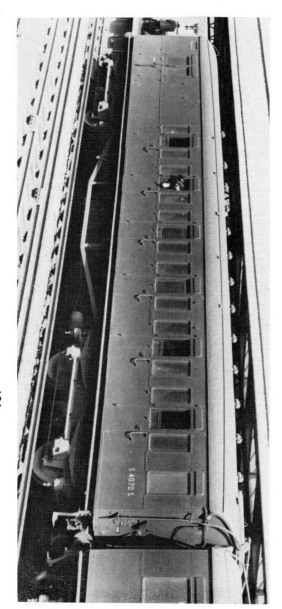

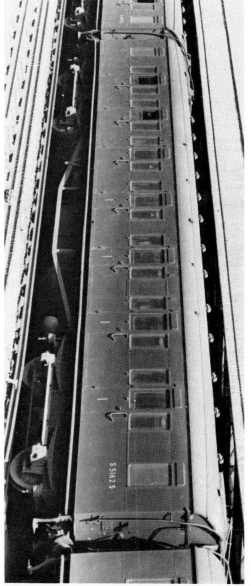

SR 1924-37
Corridor stock

When Maunsell was appointed chief mechanical engineer of the SR one of his first tasks was to design new corridor stock for SR long distance services. Because of loading gauge restrictions ranging from the severe 8ft maximum body width limit for a 60ft coach between Tunbridge Wells and Hastings, and 8ft 6in width on many of the former SE&C lines, to a general restriction elsewhere of 9ft width, Maunsell designed three widths of stock, all otherwise generally similar with steel-panelled side-door bodies. The 8ft wide coaches (restriction 0) for the Hastings line and the 8ft 6in wide coaches (restriction 1), for Thanet services, had virtually straight sides, but the wider 9ft coaches (restriction 4) had the usual tumblehome sides curving inwards below the waist. Guard's compartments on the 9ft wide coaches had recessed sides, but had look-out duckets which the narrower coaches did not have.

On page 186 are two restriction 1 coaches, at the top, a corridor composite and below a corridor brake third both part of a four-coach set. At the top of this page is a restriction 0 brake composite, and BELOW a restriction 4 brake third. On page 188, left, is a restriction 4

[Concluded on page 188

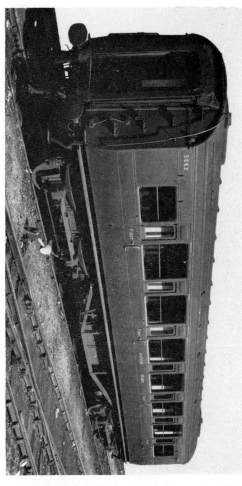

SR corridor stock
concluded

corridor composite, and BELOW a restriction 4 open third of 1936. Two types of coach built for boat train use in the early 1930s were open unclassed vehicles (non-descripts), which were labelled first, second or third as occasion demanded. Internally, seats, of virtually first class standards, were arranged one-and-two on each side of an off-central passageway. The coaches were later classified as seconds while three-class travel survived on boat trains. On the facing page, top, is a non-descript open coach and, below, the companion non-descript open brake. Notice the difference in window layout.
[G. M. Kichenside; British Railways; R. C. Riley

190

SR 1945-8
Corridor stock

Distinguishing features of SR stock designed by Bulleid were all-steel sides and ends (but not roof, which continued to be of wood and canvas construction), bodysides with a continuous curve from floor to cantrail widest at the waist, windows with pronounced curves at the corners, and toplights on doors. Bulleid's first post-war designs were 58ft side-door corridor coaches, most of which were formed into three-coach sets of two brake thirds and a composite (LEFT). From about 1947 new end-door designs appeared on 63ft 5in underframes and including such types as a semi-open brake third. BELOW is six-coach set of Bulleid stock for the Bournemouth line; TOP RIGHT is a kitchen third and, BELOW RIGHT a semi-open first.
[British Railways

SR Tavern cars 1949

Soon after nationalisation BR introduced a number of new features in train catering, particularly in the provision of buffet cars, and cafeteria cars serving light meals and snacks. Among the innovations were Tavern cars, placed in service on the Southern and Eastern Regions during the summer of 1949, intended to portray the atmosphere and style of an old English pub. Internally the cars were finished with mock-Tudor beams, oak panelling and leaded light windows; externally parts at least of the coach bodies were painted to represent red brickwork below the waist, and plaster and beams above. Southern sets were Bulleid vehicles which ran as a pair, a kitchen buffet with the saloon bar, and a dining car, which was unusual in that the two rows of seats and tables ran length ways backing the outer walls of the coach. Windows in both the dining car and saloon bar were confined to toplights, so that passengers could not see out when eating. That alone ensured their unpopularity and the cars were soon rebuilt as conventional restaurant and buffet cars.

[British Railways

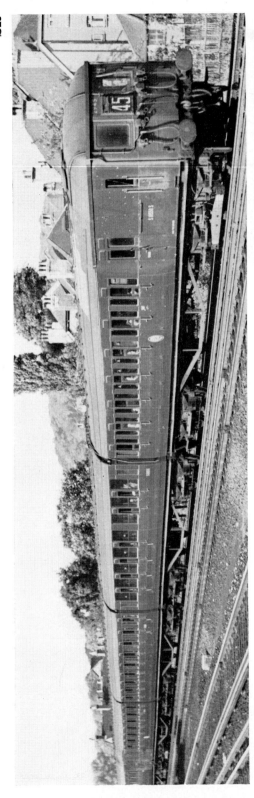

SR Electric semi-fast
4-LAV stock 1932

The electric stock built in 1932 for semi-fast and stopping services on the Southern's newly electrified Brighton line was outer suburban in character, and formed of four coaches, two non-corridor motor brake thirds, a non-corridor composite with five first and four third class compartments, and a side-corridor non-gangwayed lavatory composite, all on 62ft underframes (ABOVE). The body width was 9ft, the first electric stock of this width to run on the Southern other than the original LBSCR South London sets. The bodysides were recessed at the guard's and driver's ends of the motor coaches. A feature of the corridor composite was the arrangement of double doors (RIGHT) between the compartments and the corridor, used also in the SR express electric stock of the same period and by the LMS from 1930 onwards. The third class compartments in non-corridor coaches had armrests dividing the seating into five-a-side, as two one, and two.

[P. J. Sharpe; British Railways

193

SR Suburban Electric 1925-48

Maunsell's only new non-corridor suburban stock for the Southern was built in 1925 and consisted of two batches of three-coach electric sets for the Eastern and Western sections, generally similar in appearance, and not unlike the last of the South Eastern & Chatham 10-compartment steam-hauled thirds of a year or so before. The electric sets were 8ft 6in wide but the two batches differed in detail: Eastern Section coaches were 62ft long but units for the Western section had 60ft trailers and 56ft 11in motor coaches, the latter with V nose front ends. LEFT, is an Eastern section 62ft motor brake third.

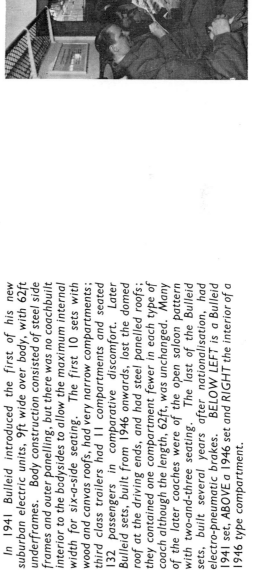

In 1941 Bulleid introduced the first of his new suburban electric units, 9ft wide over body, with 62ft underframes. Body construction consisted of steel side frames and outer panelling, but there was no coachbuilt interior to the bodysides to allow the maximum internal width for six-a-side seating. The first 10 sets with wood and canvas roofs, had very narrow compartments; third class trailers had 11 compartments and seated 132 passengers in comparative discomfort. Later Bulleid sets, built from 1946 onwards, lost the domed roof at the driving ends, and had steel panelled roofs; they contained one compartment fewer in each type of coach although the length, 62ft, was unchanged. Many of the later coaches were of the open saloon pattern with two-and-three seating. The last of the Bulleid sets, built several years after nationalisation, had electro-pneumatic brakes. BELOW LEFT is a Bulleid 1941 set, ABOVE a 1946 set and RIGHT the interior of a 1946 type compartment.

SR Electric 2-BIL and 2-HAL semi-fast 1935-9

All SR outer-suburban stock after the Brighton line 4-LAV sets consisted of two-coach units comprising a motor brake third and driving trailer composite. The units for the semi-fast and stopping services for the Hastings and Portsmouth electrifications of 1935 and 1937 had corridors in both coaches, although there were no external gangways, and were classified as 2-BIL (ABOVE). Later units of this type featured a change in construction detail, for from about 1937 window glass was inserted from the inside of the body instead of being held on the outside of the frame by wooden beading. Stock for the Maidstone and Gillingham electrification of 1939 was rather more angular with steel flush sides; only the driving trailers had corridor and toilet facilities. A 2-HAL unit is illustrated BELOW.

[British Railways

SR Electric Brighton line express 1933-5

Express sets for the Brighton and associated electrification schemes of 1932 and 1935 consisted of six-coach units with through gangways within each unit. The motor coaches were of the open saloon pattern with end doors, but the trailers were side corridor vehicles with external doors to each compartment and were generally similar to Maunsell's steam corridor stock of the time, except in length which was fixed at 62ft 6in underframes for most of the express electric coaches. The earliest units included a single composite Pullman car but later sets had instead a pantry first (BELOW) from which an attendant could serve light refreshments. The earliest motor coaches (ABOVE) had large drop windows but the later batch had fixed windows with sliding glass ventilator windows above.

[British Railways

197

Portsmouth
Stock 1937-8

Express stock for later SR main line electrification
schemes was formed into four-coach units which
differed from earlier sets by being gangwayed throughout; one set of restaurant car facilities could thus be
reached by passengers from all parts of the train.
The driving cabs of the motor coaches were fitted with
a partition door which served as the gangway door
when the cab was occupied by the driver but swung
round to shut off the cab from passenger access when
the motor coach was in the middle of the train. LEFT
is a Portsmouth 1937 motor saloon brake third and,
BELOW, a trailer composite.

[British Railways

SR Electric 1937-8 Refreshment cars

The four-coach units, opposite, were delivered in two batches, in 1937 for the Waterloo-Portsmouth service and in 1938 for the Victoria-Bognor/Portsmouth service. The catering differed on the two services; Waterloo-Portsmouth trains included a kitchen third and semi-open first restaurant unit which served full a la carte meals. RIGHT is the interior of the kitchen third. The Bognor service had buffet cars, arranged internally with a long buffet counter with bar stool seats and four four-seat tables at one end (BELOW). The Bognor buffets were the first Southern coaches to be turned out in Malachite green livery. In a stock reshuffle in the early 1960s some of the Portsmouth restaurant sets were sent to the Brighton line and acquired Pullman cars in place of the kitchen thirds; meanwhile the Bognor buffet sets were transferred to the Waterloo-Portsmouth line.
[British Railways

199

Metropolitan stock 1890-1900

Metropolitan carriages in the latter part of the 19th century included four- and rigid eight-wheelers, but from 1898 the Metropolitan introduced bogie stock built by the Ashbury C & W Co. The coaches were about 38ft long and 8ft wide over body. From 1905 much of the Ashbury stock was converted to electric operation. Six coaches later reverted to steam operation as push-pull vehicles for the Chesham branch; four still exist in use on the Bluebell Railway. LEFT is a four-wheel first of 1892 and BELOW, an Ashbury stock electric driving trailer third. [London Transport

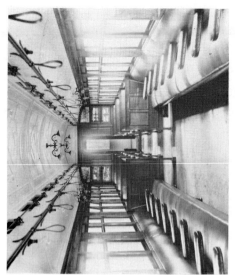

Met. 1905 Saloon electric stock

Although the Metropolitan acquired some of its electric stock by conversions from steam coaches, much was built new. The new stock of 1905 (RIGHT and BELOW) was of the open saloon pattern, with entry through end gates which were later replaced by hand-worked sliding doors. The cars themselves were rather American in appearance with domed clerestory roofs and small twin windows with inward opening toplights for ventilation. Internally the cars had longitudinal and transverse seating and ample room for standing passengers. [London Transport

201

Metropolitan 1905-21 "Dreadnoughts"

Although the first Metropolitan electrification took place in 1905 the main line from Rickmansworth to Aylesbury remained steam worked until 1961, but Aylesbury trains were hauled by electric locomotives over the electrified section of line. For its main line services the Metropolitan from 1905 onwards produced new non-corridor compartment coaches, about 51ft long and 8ft 6in wide over body, consisting of seven compartment firsts, nine compartment thirds and similar brake thirds; they had elliptical roofs and looked massive against the smaller Ashbury stock. Third class coaches were unusual in having some compartments linked in threes by a central passageway, but this feature was later abandoned. Further coaches of this type were built in 1921 and the class as a whole survived until 1961. Three still exist on the Keighley & Worth Valley Railway. *LEFT* and *BELOW* is a Dreadnought first. [London Transport

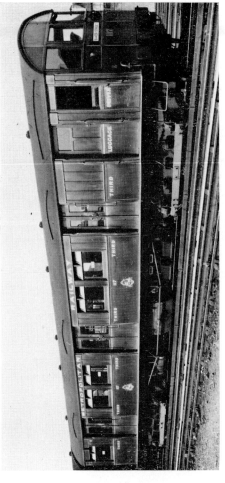

Met. 1920-32
Electric stock

Metropolitan electric stock built new until the 1920s was almost entirely of the saloon pattern; the last Metropolitan saloon stock built in the early 1920s had three sets of hand-worked sliding doors on each side of each coach to speed station stops. But from 1925 the Metropolitan introduced a new design of compartment electric stock, similar in general appearance to the Dreadnought vehicles and to two single unit motor composites of 1910, although differing in such detail as the style of body panelling. Later coaches had steel panelled sides, painted to represent graining. RIGHT is a saloon motor coach of 1921 and, BELOW, a compartment motor brake third of 1927. [LT

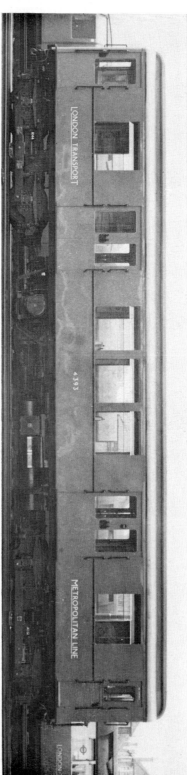

District 1905-35 Electric stock

From the start the District Railway adopted saloon type stock for its electric services from 1905; after experiments with air-operated doors hand-worked sliding end and centre doors soon became the District standard. Succeeding batches of stock differed in detail but one common feature was the clerestory roof, which the District retained to the end of its separate existence; indeed the last District-type stock was not delivered until 1936, after the formation of London Transport and was the last clerestory stock to be built for a British railway. *TOP LEFT is one of these cars on Metropolitan Line service and BELOW it a District first class trailer of 1905.* An exception to the District clerestory tradition was the 1920 stock (RIGHT and BELOW), which had elliptical roofs and distinctive oval windows at the car ends; their massive all-steel construction earned them the nick-name "tanks". During their lifetime they were the widest stock on the Underground, 9ft 6in over body.

[London Transport]

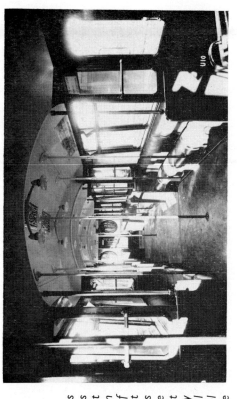

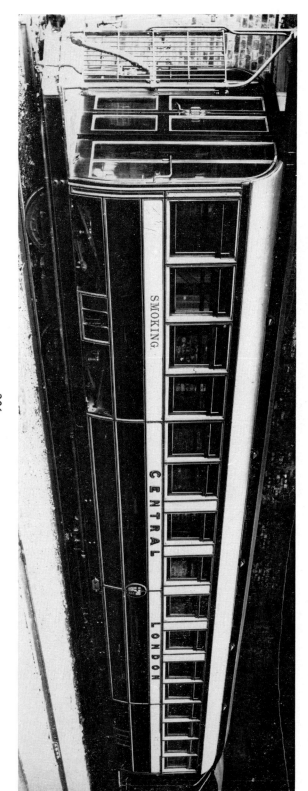

London tube stock 1907-20

Coaches for deep level tube lines in London have always been of specialised character; from the start, tube stock followed American practice with saloon interiors and open end balconies enclosed by gates, for, clearly, compartment coaches with side swing doors could not be used in the confines of a tube tunnel in case an emergency arose between stations. The first tube trains, the City & South London (1890) and the Central London Railway (1900) were locomotive-hauled; later tubes and the Waterloo & City line of 1898 had multiple-unit trains with the traction motors carried on motor coaches. TOP LEFT is a later-pattern City & South London car, BELOW LEFT, a Central London car of 1900, RIGHT, a motor car of the Hampstead tube and, BELOW, a six-car train of London & North Western and London Electric joint stock, built in 1920 for the Bakerloo service to Watford. [LPC; LT; BR

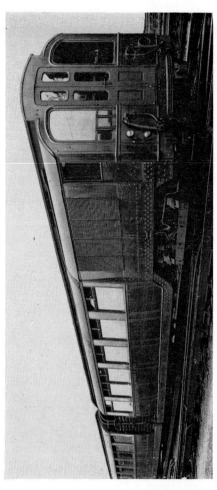

London tube stock 1923-60

From the early 1920s, after the development of reliable air-operated sliding doors, standard tube car designs were evolved; TOP LEFT is a motor car of the type built in batches between 1923 and the early 1930s; BELOW LEFT is a 1938 stock motor car, the first production tube stock to have underfloor electrical equipment; BELOW is the new standard design, built between 1959 and 1962 for the Central and Piccadilly lines, with light-weight aluminium bodies 52ft 2in long by 8ft 6in wide and 9ft 5½in high. They weigh 26½ tons in the case of the motor cars compared with the 27½ tons of the 1938 stock. RIGHT is one of the prototype motor cars built in 1960 for the Central line and now being used for experiments in automatic driving control. [LT

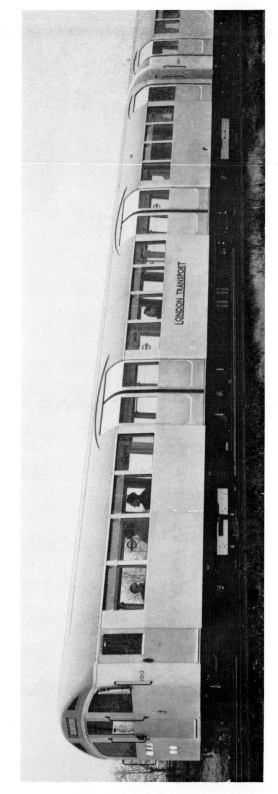

LT 1938-60
Surface stock

In 1938 London Transport introduced new saloon stock for the Metropolitan and District lines; a distinguishing feature was the skirt edge of the body which curved outwards over what would normally have been the footboards (BELOW). The first coaches of this type had steel bodies but cars built after 1947 had aluminium bodies. In 1960 LT introduced a new type of coach for Metropolitan services, the widest ever on the Underground and among the widest in Britain, 9ft 8in over body with a length of 53ft (LEFT). Light-weight motor coaches weigh no more than 32 tons compared with 34 tons of the 1938 stock.

[LT

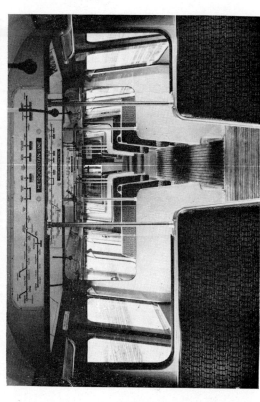

London Underground interiors 1923-60

The development of London underground stock over 70 years has inevitably brought changes in design and constructional methods. The first tube cars of 1890 were almost totally enclosed with a few small windows high up on car sides on the basis that there was nothing to see out of the windows. Present day Underground cars, in contrast, are light and airy, with plenty of windows. The first cars were largely of wooden construction which was soon frowned on because of the fire risk; steel soon replaced wood and, in recent years, aluminium has replaced steel. ABOVE LEFT is the interior of a 1923 tube stock motor car, ABOVE RIGHT a 1960 motor car for comparison and BELOW RIGHT a Metropolitan line 1960 car showing the two-and-three-seating.

[London Transport]

Liverpool Overhead Railway

The LOR, opened in 1893, was electrically-worked from the start with multiple-unit trains; weight restrictions and sharp curves necessitated coaches of light weight. LOR stock was delivered in batches, generally similar but differing in detail and in dimensions; lengths varied between 40 and 45ft and widths were 8ft 6in or 9ft 4in; seating capacities varied considerably. Open saloon interiors with side swing doors at intervals along the coach were adopted. In the last years of the line, which closed in 1956, some of the trains were rebuilt with aluminium panelled bodies, air-operated sliding doors and upholstered instead of wooden third class seats. LEFT, is one of the original trains, and BELOW one of the modernised trains.
[C. P. Boocock

Mersey Railway
Electric stock

Liverpool's other independent railway, the Mersey, was originally steam worked but was the first line in the country to be converted to electric traction. Its first electric cars were similar to the 1905 saloon cars of the Metropolitan, with clerestory roofs and end entrance vestibules enclosed by gates. Straight matchboarded sides and the small windows gave the cars a distinctly American appearance. Later the end entrances were closed in and inward-opening swing doors replaced the gates. Later stock from 1923 onwards had domed elliptical roofs and larger windows with toplight ventilator windows. BELOW is a Mersey first class driving trailer of 1925 and, RIGHT, the interior of a third class trailer of the same period.
[British Railways

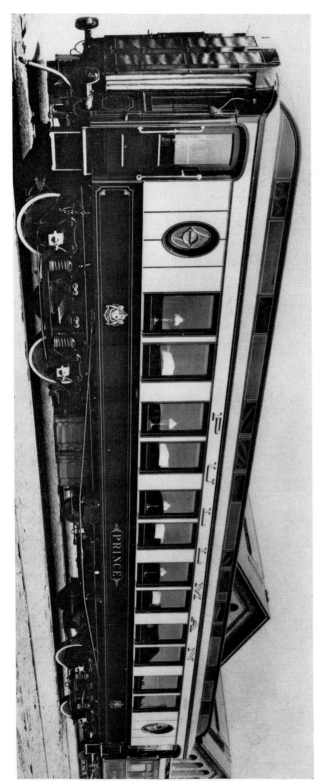

Pullman cars 1879-1910

From their introduction in Britain in the 1870s Pullmans became a symbol of luxury travel. In 1879 a Pullman car Prince of Wales rebuilt with a kitchen was placed in service on the Great Northern as the first British dining car. Later it was bought by the GN (TOP LEFT). One of the Brighton line Pullmans, Prince, BELOW LEFT, had a small pantry and was one of the first buffet cars; it was also notable for having enclosed end vestibules and gangways. Early in the present century, Pullman cars were in use on several railways; from 1910 even the Metropolitan ran Pullmans on its Aylesbury and Chesham lines, a service which lasted until 1939. Two cars were provided, May-flower and Galatea, non-gangwayed and slightly smaller than other cars with a length of 57ft 6in. Cooking was by paraffin stove. RIGHT and BELOW is Galatea.

[British Railways, London Transport

215

Pullmans - 1951 "Golden Arrow"

For the Festival of Britain in 1951 a new Pullman train was placed in service for the "Golden Arrow", consisting of two second and eight first class cars, all 62ft 4in long over headstocks and 8ft 5½in wide over body. The cars were basically similar to traditional Pullman designs but were steel panelled and included steel framing in the bodies and roofs. Underframes were, however, of LNER pattern with Gresley bogies, and the car bodies differed from previous Pullmans in having rectangular instead of oval windows in the toilets. BELOW is first class kitchen car Aquila, and LEFT the interior of first class parlour and bar, Pegasus.
[Pullman Car Co.]

Pullmans Extraordinary

In 1947 the new all-Pullman train the "Devon Belle", included a Pullman observation car (RIGHT). Two observations cars were provided for the service, rebuilt from older cars; both had a bar at the inner end. When the "Devon Belle" ceased to run the observation cars were stored but in recent years have been used for privately organised special trains and were later restored to service as observation cars in Scotland. Pullman car Malaga (BELOW), although withdrawn from service in the early 1960s has been given a fresh lease of life—as an office boardroom; it has been bought by the publisher of this book, Ian Allan Ltd, and stands at Shepperton on its own track with direct gangway access from the office building.
[Pullman Car Co.; G. M. Kichenside

Pullmans - 1933 "Brighton Belle"

The Pullman tradition of the Brighton line continued after electrification in 1933 when a new all-electric multiple-unit Pullman train was placed in service for the then named "Southern Belle" soon renamed "Brighton Belle". Three five-car trains were built, two for service and the third spare, in rotation. Each unit included two kitchen firsts, a parlour third and two third class parlour motor coaches, and each five car unit was gangwayed within the set but not at the driving ends. The train was the only electric multiple-unit Pullman in the world. Internally the third class cars differed from locomotive-hauled Pullmans in having seats two-and-two on each side of the passageway instead of the normal Pullman two-and-one arrangement. A ten car train is seen here near Merstham.

[British Railways

Budd
"Silver Princess" 1947

In 1947 an unusual coach, built by the Budd Company of America, took to the rails in Britain, and for a time in Ireland, to demonstrate constructional features new to British practice. The coach, named the Silver Princess, 63ft long, 9ft 2in wide and weighing 29 tons, was of all-steel construction and distinguished by corrugated side and roof panels. The outer skin was of stainless steel and the coach was originally unpainted. As built it was a first and third class composite, the former in side-corridor compartments, the latter in an open saloon with twin reclining and rotating seats. It ran experimentally on both the LMS and LNER and, with 5ft 3in gauge bogies, on the CIE in Ireland. Later it was allocated to the London Midland Region of BR, and upgraded to a full first. Still later, the first class compartments were replaced by a lounge-bar. RIGHT is the interior of the saloon and, BELOW, the coach as liveried in BR crimson lake and cream.

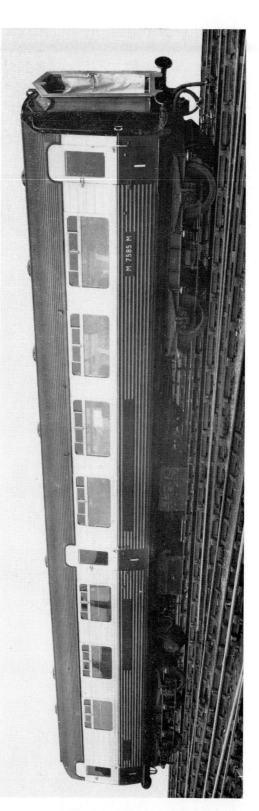

M 7585 M

BR Standard stock 1951

In 1951 British Railways produced its first standard coaches for use on all regions. Corridor coaches were on 63ft 5in underframes, with bodies 64ft 6in long and 9ft 3in wide over door handles. Non-gangwayed stock was generally on 56ft 11in underframes although some non-gangwayed vehicles were on the longer type of underframe. Corridor stock included both open and side corridor vehicles while non-gangwayed types included open coaches, some of which had toilet facilities. BELOW is a corridor third and LEFT a 56ft 11in open lavatory third.

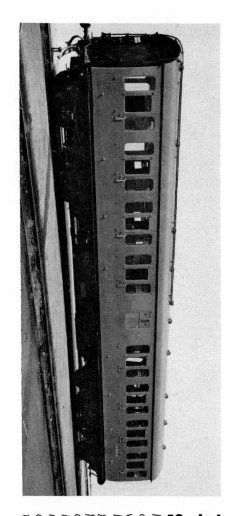

British Railways
Diesel multiple-units

An important aspect of the British Railways modernisation programme, started in the mid-1950s, was the widespread use of multiple-unit diesel trains, which have progressively taken over many stopping, semi-fast and express services. Diesel trains, like earlier locomotive-hauled coaches, were built for specific types of service; thus some units, non-gangwayed and without toilet facilities, were built for suburban use. Many units were formed into two-car sets, and included toilet facilities; they are employed on a variety of workings ranging from local services to express duty. Illustrated RIGHT is the interior of a second class car of a general-purpose unit built by British Railways, and, BELOW, a two-car unit, built by Cravens Ltd., one of several contractors who supplied many BR diesel units.
[British Railways

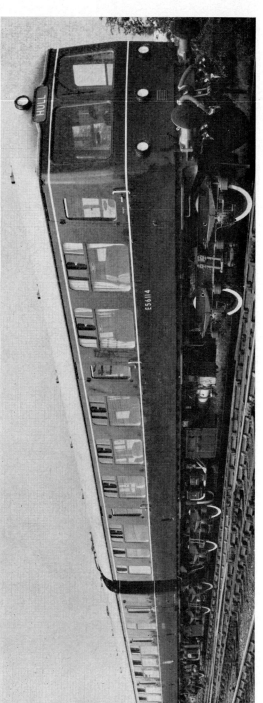

British Railways
SR and ER electrics 1949-56

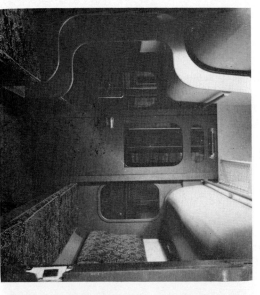

In 1949 two projects came to fruition which had been planned before nationalisation by the LNE and Southern railways. Most important was the electrification of LNER suburban services between Liverpool Street and Shenfield, which today form part of the complex Great Eastern line electrification between Liverpool Street, Southend, Clacton and Bishops Stortford. The stock for the new Shenfield services, which operated on 1,500 volts d.c. from overhead catenary, consisted of three-car units, which normally worked as nine-car trains, of the open saloon pattern with air-operated sliding doors (TOP RIGHT). For the extension of electrification to Southend in 1956, BR placed in service four-car electric units of the side-door suburban type on 63ft 5in underframes, with compartment and saloon accom-

modation and with toilet facilities (RIGHT BELOW). In 1960 both types of unit were converted for high voltage a.c. electrification. Also in 1949 the Southern completed two four-car double-deck suburban electric units which normally ran as a pair. (BELOW) They were not true double-deckers, for the high and low level compartments were interlaced; access to the high level compartments was by a short staircase from an adjacent low level compartment. Seating capacity of the eight car train was 1,104 compared with 772 in a conventional train. But the double deckers were not a success, for they lost time at stations; although they are still in service no more have been built and train capacity on the SR was increased by the provision of longer trains.

[British Railways

222

BR suburban electrics 1960-5

On page 223 is illustrated one of the earlier BR standard four-coach outer suburban multiple-units; on this page, are two of the more recent types, BELOW, a three-car set for Glasgow area suburban services, with saloon interiors, air operated sliding doors, and bodies 3in wider than normal; LEFT is one of the latest units for Euston-Rugby-Birmingham semi-fast services. The side-door arrangement has been perpetuated but the front end design has been improved with curved windscreens. The LMR units are partly gangwayed the coaches are of integral construction and ride almost silently.

[British Railways

British Railways express electrics

Although standard locomotive-hauled main-line coach designs have been evolved for all regions, multiple-unit express electric units, while conforming in general body style to standard patterns, differ in interior layouts and in front end design. The Southern has always favoured the rather flat, austere front, and even its latest Brighton line stock (BELOW) retains this rather uninspiring front end, relieved only by curved corners. The express stock for the Liverpool Street–Clacton service, however, has a wrap-round windscreen, rather like the Glasgow units, opposite, but interrupted by the gangway connection (RIGHT).

[B. A. Haresnape; British Railways

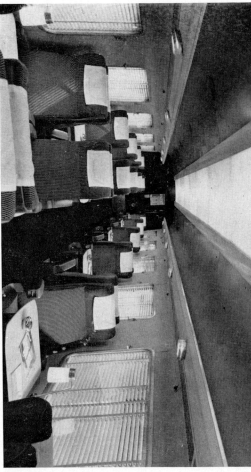

BR
Diesel Pullmans

Full air-conditioning, double-glazed windows, venetian blinds, sound insulation and partly reclining seats were features of new all-Pullman diesel multiple-units built for the Western and London Midland Regions in 1960. Indeed, these Pullmans were quite unlike any other Pullmans that had ever run in Britain, for the general styling and decor resulted from designs prepared by a team of industrial designers. In striking blue and white livery, the diesel Pullmans, set a new standard in British railway travelling facilities. LEFT, is the interior of a first class saloon and, BELOW, one of the eight-car WR diesel Pullmans.

[British Railways

BR XP64
and the future

In 1964 BR introduced prototype coaches embodying new design features in order to assess their value for future standard coaches. New bogies of a simpler pattern but giving an improved and quieter ride, new seat profiles, larger windows, and wider doors and entrance vestibules are some of the ideas on trial. Integral construction, to reduce weight, will be employed on future designs, although the experimental XP64 train was of the conventional pattern with independent underframe. RIGHT is the interior of an open second class saloon; BELOW is an open second with folding doors. The latter are likely to be replaced by sliding doors in future designs. [British Railways

Independent narrow gauge stock

In view of the perilous state of narrow gauge railways a few years ago it seems incredible that new narrow gauge coaches should be placed in service in 1965. Yet the 2ft 3in gauge Talyllyn and 1ft 11½in gauge Festiniog railways, both rescued from extinction by preservation societies are building new stock. BELOW LEFT, is the new Festiniog first and third class composite. ABOVE LEFT is one of the earliest Festiniog bogie composites dating from the late 1870s and carefully

restored. BELOW RIGHT is an original four-wheel third of the Talyllyn Railway dating from 1866. ABOVE is a coach from the Romney, Hythe & Dymchurch, one of Britain's two smallest public railways, with a 15in-gauge. The early RHDR enclosed bogie coaches were styled after Gresley's LNER stock, but later coaches had only two instead of three compartments and were flush sided.
[P. J. Sharpe; R. Ransome-Wallis; Festiniog Railway

By the same author

British Railways Coaches

British Railway Signalling

Veteran & Vintage Railway Carriages

Railway Carriage Album